In *Fit for Your Assignment* Pastor Reina Olmeda beautifully and masterfully weaves together personal experiences, biblical teachings, and her deep passion for God as she creates an essential resource for readers yearning to be physically, mentally, and spiritually balanced and ready to serve and live life faithfully. Her four-step method of conviction, confrontation, revelation, and transformation provides a strong theological grounding and compassionate push to get us moving together on this holistic journey. The thirty-day fitness plan—a delectable mix of challenge, encouragement, practical wisdom, and prayer—will transform not only those bold enough to walk this journey but also everyone they meet!

—Rev. Dr. Deborah Appler
Associate professor, Hebrew Bible,
Moravian Theological Seminary

The current mental, physical, and spiritual health matters of our world should be of great concern to us all. In times such as this influential voices are allowed access to the airways to address the matters at hand. *Fit for Your Assignment* is designed to provoke its readers to reconsideration and realignment. The pen of Pastor Reina has moved on the pages herein with a passion birthed out of personal experience. This tremendous tool will serve as the catalyst for lifestyle changes sure to rob the grave of far too many early committals and bankrupt the thieves of destiny.

—Wynell Freeman
Free Man Ministries

Fit for Your Assignment is a perfect title for a book that affirms that you were not an accident. "Before I formed you in the womb I knew you" (Jer. 1:5). God knew you before you were even born. What an amazing thought! He saw your unformed substance and said, "I have a purpose for this life. I have good plans for them." You have been handpicked by almighty God to be here at this time in history!

The author of this book shares some valuable principles that she has lived and experienced and now for such a time as this would like them to impact your life and the world. It's important have a healthy rounded life to impact others.

Remember, He knew you before you were ever born! Find confidence in His love, knowing that you are a person of destiny and are part of His mighty plan! Congrats to Pastor Reina Olmeda, who has fitted her own assignment in the kingdom, and it's leading others to fit theirs.

—REV. MANUEL A. ALVAREZ
Superintendent, Assemblies of God Spanish Eastern District

Fit for Your Assignment is not just another in a long line of self-help books. It is a deeply spiritual work that will take every reader on a journey of transformation that will make them feel and live better. This is a powerful, approachable work that reminds us that we have been created for a very specific purpose, but that purpose can be thwarted until you are spiritually, mentally, and physically fit for what God planned for you. As a Christian educator I have seen firsthand how critical a whole-person approach to health can be. This book will help believers understand the seamlessness between the spiritual and the physical, making you whole and ready to fulfill your calling.

—CARLOS CAMPOS, PhD
President, Alliance for Hispanic Education/NHCLC

fit *for* YOUR assignment

fit *for* YOUR assignment

●●●

REINA OLMEDA

SILOAM

Most CHARISMA HOUSE BOOK GROUP products are available at special quantity discounts for bulk purchase for sales promotions, premiums, fund-raising, and educational needs. For details, write Charisma House Book Group, 600 Rinehart Road, Lake Mary, Florida 32746, or telephone (407) 333-0600.

FIT FOR YOUR ASSIGNMENT by Reina Olmeda
Published by Siloam
Charisma Media/Charisma House Book Group
600 Rinehart Road
Lake Mary, Florida 32746
www.charismahouse.com

Cover design by Lisa Rae Cox
Design Director: Bill Johnson

Visit the author's website at www.reinaolmeda.com.

Library of Congress Cataloging-in-Publication Data:
An application to register this book for cataloging has been submitted to the Library of Congress.
International Standard Book Number: 978-1-62136-612-6
E-book ISBN: 978-1-62136-613-3

Neither the publisher nor the author is engaged in rendering professional advice or services to the individual reader. The ideas, procedures, and suggestions in this book are not intended as a substitute for consulting with your physician. All matters regarding your health require medical supervision. Neither the author nor the publisher shall be liable or responsible for any loss or damage allegedly arising from any information or suggestion in this book.

While the author has made every effort to provide accurate telephone numbers and Internet addresses at the time of publication, neither the publisher nor the author assumes any responsibility for errors or for changes that occur after publication.

This publication is translated in Spanish under the title *Aptos para su mission*, copyright © 2014 by Reina Olmeda, published by Casa Creación, a Charisma Media company. All rights reserved.

First edition

14 15 16 17 18 — 9 8 7 6 5 4 3 2 1
Printed in the United States of America

I Dedicate This Book to

My Lord and Savior, Jesus Christ—in You I live, move, and have my being. Truly Your Word never returns void!

My best friend and love of my life, my husband, Charles. You have been one of the greatest God winks I have been given. Your unconditional love and your passion for excellence have challenged me to become greater and wiser. Your "pleasant words are like a honeycomb, sweetness to the soul and health to the bones" (Prov. 16:24, NKJV). For every moment spent making me shine bright, for all the time and effort spent walking this journey alongside of me, I thank you! Words are not enough to express how much I truly love you. You have been my greatest supporter, my better half, cheering me on every step of our journey. Your time and expertise were so valuable to me as you became my second pair of eyes and the voice of reason during this season in my life. Thank you so much for loving me and believing in me. Thank you for dreaming with me and for reminding me of my assignment every day. You are a godly man of great character and integrity, a wonderful husband, an amazing father, and I get to spend my life with you. I will forever love you, my Charlie!

My two beautiful princesses, Amberly and Andrea. Your births undoubtedly changed my life in ways too great to enumerate. Thank you for reminding me every day of my assignment as your mommy! Your unconditional love serves to fuel my passion to live my life in a way you can emulate. I know that whatever I have accomplished thus far and have yet to accomplish, you girls will go further and do greater.

My amazing parents, Sam and Elizabeth, the greatest and most loving parents. Oh, how I love you so. Thank you both for instructing me in the ways of the Lord. Look what the Lord has done! Dad, you are and forever will be my handsome Superman. Your life has been the perfect example of what God can do with a man who surrenders wholeheartedly to God. Mom, you are beautiful, wise, and passionate about God and family. You are my Wonder Woman. You are the perfect example of the Proverbs 31 woman. I am so proud to say, "I am my mother's daughter." Thank you both for showing me that nothing is impossible for those who trust in the Lord. *¡Los amo con todo mi corazón!*

My brother, Rev. Sam Rodriguez. You are my Elijah. You are a man of great anointing, influence, and integrity. You have inspired me to be more and do more. I am so thankful to God for you. Your unconditional love, prayers, and words of wisdom have blessed me beyond measure. I love being your big sister, and for the record you will never stop being "Bosley." Thank you for believing in me. I love you forever!

My beautiful sister, Lizzette. You are fearless, strong, courageous, inspiring, and loving. I am so blessed to have you in my life. Simply by your presence you know how to change an atmosphere in a room. Through happy, funny, sad, and serious moments you have been my faithful and unshakable friend. Thank you for your prayers and for believing in me. Thank you for taking time out of your busy schedule to help me when I needed you. I have the most amazing sister in the world. I love you, "chun fui."

My other amazing sister, Eva. Thank you for being an incredible cheerleader throughout my accomplishments and for believing in me. From the rides to college to where we are today, all I can say is God is faithful. I love you, Evita!

CONTENTS

SECTION ONE
ARE YOU FIT FOR YOUR ASSIGNMENT?

SECTION TWO
THE FOUR PRINCIPLES OF GETTING
FIT FOR YOUR ASSIGNMENT

SECTION THREE
FINISHING WELL

SECTION FOUR
THE FIT FOR YOUR ASSIGNMENT THIRTY-DAY CHALLENGE

ACKNOWLEDGMENTS

I WANT TO START by acknowledging my Third Day Worship Center family and staff. I am so honored to serve you. What an amazing church God has blessed me with. Thank you for your prayers, support, and love. Your "Pastora" loves you beyond words.

To the Fit for Your Assignment group, you ladies have inspired me in more ways than you will ever know. Thank you for being transparent and for keeping me accountable when I needed it most. We are in this journey together.

To Liz Gonzalez, Jewel Davis, and Cindy Ruiz, who took time out of their busy schedules to help me get through a very stressful weekend. I could not have done it all without you.

A great big thank-you to Janet Rivera for being such a faithful friend and servant. Thank you for loving my girls. Your efforts have not gone unnoticed. God will reward you abundantly.

Thank you to the armor bearers for your love and dedication to the ministry. We are blessed to have each of you in your lives. Jessica Colmenares, your personal commitment to the assignment over my life is noticed. You are such a blessing. Your "Boaz" will have a great assignment over his life. Jessica Gonzalez, my traveling and anointed interpreter, thank you for making this assignment yours. I'm always happy to share my snacks with you.

I can't forget my amazing actresses and actors (you know who you are) who spent time ensuring that the message delivered would be projected with an excellence spirit. You all get an Academy Award as far as I am concerned! Jason Velasquez, thank you for investing your time, skills, and expertise. You are truly gifted, and I know the best is yet to come.

Thank you to those who I had the amazing opportunity to interview for this project. Your transparency and stories will touch and serve helpful in changing many lives.

Finally I want to thank Charisma House for giving me the opportunity to bring forth this message to the masses. Debbie Marrie, Tessie DeVore, Jevon Bolden, Woodley Auguste, and the rest of the Charisma House staff, thank you for your excellent service and commitment. May God continue to enlarge your territory. Margarita Henry, what can I say; you are truly a godsend. You have been a true and inspirational blessing in my life. Thank you for embracing this message as your own. I pray many God winks your way!

FOREWORD

OUR FAITH IS not like any other faith. Our faith is transparent, transcendent, and transformational. Our faith teaches us to cross over obstacles, shout down walls, break through crowds, and walk on water, even in the midst of storms.

Our faith enables us to survive the fires of life, overcome the den of lions, silence the serpents, and outwit the fox. Our faith empowers us to see the invisible, embrace the impossible, and hope for the incredible.

Accordingly it is not a coincidence that the first time the universe heard God's voice, He did not say let there be joy, peace, or even love. The voice of the sovereign, the divine, the glorious uttered the following: "Let there be light!" (Gen. 1:3).

God always begins by turning on the lights.

Life requires light.

Faith requires light.

Why? We cannot deny the fact we live in dark times. Some argue that we live in the darkest hour, darkened by sin, immorality, moral relativism, spiritual apathy, cultural decadence, infanticide, racism, pornography, poverty, false prophets, watered-down preaching, hypocrisy, unbridled consumerism, voyeurism, materialism, secular tyranny, discord, division, strife, hatred, jealousy, and unbelief.

Yet in the midst of darkness stems a prophetic truth, a revealed truth, an everlasting truth uttered by our Savior:

> You are the light of the world. A city on a hill cannot be hidden. Neither do people light a lamp and put it under a

bowl. Instead they put it on its stand, and it gives light to everyone in the house. In the same way, let your light shine before men, that they may see your good deeds and praise your Father in heaven.

—MATTHEW 5:14–16

In order to shine the light and change the world, we must embrace the following admonitions. First, today's complacency is tomorrow's captivity. Second, spiritual stagnation always leads to moral atrophy. Third, truth must never be sacrificed on the altar of expediency.

Accordingly a question must be asked requiring an encounter with tangential sensitivity to the voice of God's Spirit. Corresponding query goes beyond desire, commitment, passion, or inclination to "be light." The query, a simple one, stands as follows: Are we fit to shine the light? Are we fit to speak truth to power? Are we fit to confront the pathetic with the prophetic and fight the good fight? Are we fit to shine on the proverbial stand of God's Word and overcome darkness by the blood of the Lamb? Are we fit for the assignment?

To that regard, my early years of development in response to my God-ordained assignment required a rigorous regimen and processes that equipped me for today's reality. When God called me to be light, He surrounded me and continues to surround me with loving instructors committed to making sure I stand "fit" for my assignment.

One of the most prominent trainers and "workout partners" in my journey is none other than the author of this book, my sister Reina Olmeda. This modern-day Deborah prayed, worked, pushed, healed, motivated, and inspired me to be "fit" for my assignment.

As one of the most important voices in the kingdom, Pastor Reina carries an anointing that will enable Christ followers to respond with an unbridled yes to the aforementioned query. This revelation will enable every reader, without exception, to be fit to shine the light of Christ and fulfill their corresponding God-ordained mission.

For at the end of the day, fitness requires action. Just as Jesus changed the world via the conduit of His character, rhetoric, and actions, so can we edify a firewall of righteousness and justice, reform the culture, and push back the darkness by being fit for our assignments.

It takes conviction to repent, courage to speak truth, holiness to see God, faith to move mountains, and a fit mind, body, soul, and spirit to change the world!

Fit to change the world!

—Rev. Dr. Samuel Rodriguez Jr.
President, Hispanic Evangelical Association

INTRODUCTION

I REMEMBER THE DAY vividly! It was a beautiful April afternoon. The sun was bright, and the breeze blowing through my window brought a sense of newness and hope. I was in high spirits as I prepared to minister at a women's conference later that evening. I was going to dress in a recently purchased pair of tan slacks and a long blue shirt. I envisioned myself looking fabulous and ready to walk in my assignment. In my mind I looked professional and ministerial, and a thin woman stood at the center of my conscience. I got dressed and made the infamous walk to the mirror.

I have often heard that what people most often see in the mirror is a reflection of their own created and perceived ideal self. Perhaps I was one of those people. I was not prepared to see with such precision the consequences poor choices and actions had made. I looked absolutely ridiculous! The pants were too tight, and the blouse appeared two sizes smaller. I told myself, "This could not be!"

Without hesitation I walked away from the mirror and chose to believe what I had envisioned in my mind rather than what I had seen in the mirror. At that moment I did not realize the Spirit of God had begun to stir something within me. God decided He was going to thrust me into my purpose and destiny via a difficult and arduous process that would take me on a journey of conviction, confrontation, revelation, and transformation.

I asked myself, "When did I give God permission to walk into my life and pull me out of my comfort zone?" Ah, yes! It was New Year's Eve, when under a powerful move of God in my church, I prayed:

Lord, this coming year will be different. I need to see every word that has been declared over my life come to pass. Lord, have Your way with me. Whatever You ask of me, I will do. I will even get on an airplane and fly wherever You want me to go and speak Your message. [Yes, I had a fear of flying.] Everything that needs to change, I will change, Lord, because this is my year.

What I did not know at that moment was that I was about to embark upon a journey that would transform not only my life but others' as well. And in the process it would make me completely fit for my assignment.

This book is about God's desire to make you wholly and completely fit for your assignment. His desire is for you to be joyful, fulfilled, and in optimal health—spiritually, mentally, and physically. Through the lens of Scripture and personal experiences, as well as testimonies from individuals who have been transformed, you will discover the power of obedience and surrender. You will possess an understanding that as a child of God you have a unique assignment that only you can fulfill. The more fit you are, the further you will go.

Fit for Your Assignment will take you through a four-step process: conviction, confrontation, revelation, and transformation. The Spirit of God will begin to expose those areas in your life that have been neglected. As you begin to take inventory of your life, God will reveal areas that are unbalanced and unhealthy.

Step 1: Conviction

As you allow the Spirit of God to work, you will be convicted and empowered to move forward on your journey. I realized that the more I engaged in ministry and became increasingly known and recognized, the more pressure I felt to meet the expectations of others. Rather than submitting my concerns, battles, and fears to God, I caved to bad eating habits. In an effort to evade negative emotions, stress, and fears, I became a procrastinator and found myself keeping busy in the everyday routines rather than pursuing God's assignment and destiny for my life. However, God loves me so much that He does not allow me—or you—to wallow in sorrows and defeats.

When conviction made me realize I was not fit for the assignment God had for my life, a sudden sense of urgency exploded within me. I knew I had to change. I was no longer comfortable. Something was happening to me. Everything I thought I had been doing right suddenly seemed so wrong. I felt disconnected from self, family, ministry, and God. The voice of conviction was speaking, and its truth was compelling.

We live in a fast-paced society. The voices clamoring for our attention seem to be never ending. From work responsibilities to ministry duties, house chores to family time, and public advertisements to technology and social media, there is an ongoing demand for our attention. In the process, however, time for self-analysis and wholeness takes a backseat to the other driving forces.

Allow me to speak some hope into this vicious cycle. As you allow conviction to set in via the conduit of your time with God, you will sense an awareness of those areas that lack attention. Conviction awakens an awareness of sin, which prompts a need for repentance. When repentance is active, cleansing is inevitable. You may ask, "Sin?" Well, "it is a sin when someone knows the right thing to do and doesn't do it" (James 4:17, CEB).

The moment you are enlightened, via the power of conviction, to those areas of your life that need careful attention, things will begin to change for the better. You will begin to think with clarity. As a result you will begin to mentally and spiritually address things you may have put on the back burner. God will provide clarity of mind as a result of your willingness to align yourself with His purpose.

You will begin to be enlightened in areas that you previously dismissed as "part of everyday living." You will begin to realize that in order for you to be optimally aligned to God's assignment for your life, your body (and what you feed it) needs purposeful care. You no longer eat as a result of stress, life on the run, or leisure. You eat purposefully as part of your conviction.

All of these changes are inevitably intertwined to who you are spiritually. Have you ever had a rather big, delicious, overindulgent meal right before a worship service, Bible class, or prayer time? The result? A cry for the Lord to help you deal with the overwhelming feeling of lethargy creeping into your body, mind, and spirit. OK, maybe you haven't experienced that, but I certainly have.

Conviction will cause your spirit to be attuned to not only the things we normally categorize as "spiritual"—prayer, worship, church attendance, and the like—but also to every area of your life that makes up your spiritual wholeness and makes you effective in your assignment. We have to get this: We are not compartmentalized. We are whole beings with a spirit, mind, and body that are interconnected and operate in unison.

How you physically treat your body affects how you mentally respond to the spiritual nature of who you are. How you are spiritually attuned to the Spirit of God reflects in how you are able to serve Him and others physically and emotionally. Your mental alertness in responding to life's ups and downs is directly connected to your physical wellness and spiritual intimacy with God. You will have the mind of Christ. Do you see what I mean? You cannot be well in one area and think that you will be fit for the long haul of your assignment. Everything must be aligned.

How wonderful that your health will improve, your body will demonstrate it, your mind with think with clarity, and your spirit will be at peace. Conviction is what brings this about. Is it worth the time and investment? You tell me. How valuable is your assignment?

Step 2: Confrontation

This book will explore how confrontation will lead you to expose areas of your life that are wearing you down. Your obedience and willingness to deal with the situation will bring these areas under God's control.

Confrontation for me came like a tsunami hitting the shore at a speed too fast to escape its force, lifting and displacing everything I kept neatly organized and tucked away in the secret compartment of my soul. The silence of the aftermath was shattered by a very familiar voice that spoke to the core of my heart, "I love you, and I want so much more for you, but you are going to have to join Me and confront all areas in your life that are controlling you."

When was the last time you combed your hair, ironed your clothing and dressed appropriately, and put on makeup or, if you are a man, shaved nicely, simply because you were going to speak to someone over the telephone? If you are anything like me, there are some mornings where the professionalism in my voice and what the person on the other end would see if they were able to see me via sound waves are on complete opposite sides of the spectrum. Why? It's simple. I can project a professional version of myself effectively because I am not face-to-face with the person on the other end of the phone call. And the person on the other line cannot judge me on the basis of my appearance.

One of the definitions of confrontation is "the state of being confronted, especially a meeting face to face."[1] Now that changes everything. With this type of confrontation, there is little or no room to hide. This is what God does once conviction arises and we are confronted with those things we were accustomed to hiding.

Don't worry, there is no need to fear. When God confronts you through His Word and through that voice that speaks to your spirit about those things that are out of place, He does it because He already has the answers to how you can fix those hidden areas.

Confrontation will realign your thinking with who God created you to be. It will allow you to come face-to-face with those mental, physical, and spiritual areas you thought you could hide. What you didn't realize is that you were not hiding from anyone at all. Perhaps in the physical, you may have thought that if you could hide it from people, then everything would be fine. But the truth is, you were only misleading yourself. You see, confrontation is about self. It was never about what people saw. It was always about what you thought you could hide from yourself. When confrontation sets in, you will be able to look at yourself, be honest with yourself, and begin your journey to a greater revelation.

Step 3: Revelation

As you move forward in your journey, through the lens of Scripture you will receive revelation. This revelation will prompt you to realize that it is not enough to "like" you; you must "love" you. Loving you means you take care of "you"! Scripture says, "'Love the Lord your God with all your heart and with all your soul and with all your strength and with all your mind,' and 'Love your neighbor as yourself'" (Luke 10:27). Loving yourself means taking time to invest in self-care in all areas of your life.

The revelation of God's Word is the light that makes clear the darkened paths of your life. The psalmist writes, "Your word is a lamp to my feet and a light to my path" (Ps. 119:105, NKJV). Confrontation can be detrimental if you don't have the guiding light of God's Word to reveal the journey you need to take and the path to correction.

I often recommend to people (it's a nonnegotiable in my life) to take time to meditate on God's Word. Whether you are engaged in personal devotions, a group Bible study, or even notes from your church's worship service, take the time to meditate on what you've read or heard. Once you allow yourself to soak in what you have received, conviction will set in, and confrontation will enlighten you, but it is the revelation of God's Word that will show you *how* to make it applicable to those specific areas of your life.

It is interesting how Psalm 119:105 depicts the functionality of the light. It doesn't project it as a massive light source illuminating a broad area. It projects it as a light making clear the path right before you. Let me suggest that God's Word serves as the light that brings revelation to whatever circumstance you may need to address—step by step.

As you allow this revelation to illuminate your path and you become proactive in following the leading of this revelation, the time will come when you will symbolically look back at the road traveled and realize that your mind, body, and spirit have been aligned to God's purpose.

Step 4: Transformation

Lastly, this book will lead you to transformation! You will walk in full awareness that God reigns over your life. You will learn to live with daily dependency on God for all choices and decisions you make. As God demonstrates His love for you, you will walk in your assignment. You will be fit to walk in the fullness of all that has been destined for you. You will step into a new life, a life that will lead you to the fulfillment of your greatest mission, purpose, and destiny!

When our church bought our first ministry building, it was an eighty-year-old structure. It had been built as a belt and accessories manufacturing facility. We learned from the factory's former employees (who later become members of our church) that in its heyday, it was very active, functional, and productive facility. However, for the vision we had, it would no longer work. Were we going to tear it down? Absolutely not! The "bone structure" was great. We could certainly work with it, but a total transformation was going to be necessary if the functionality of it was going to meet our current and future vision.

Please understand me. Who you are or have been may not necessary be completely inadequate. Like our building, perhaps you were aligned and functional to fill a particular assignment at a given time. But based on where God is taking you *now* and the purposes He has for you *now*, are you aligned and functional? I can unashamedly tell you that in my case I was not. I needed to be transformed in my thinking, health and eating habits, and spiritual disciplines.

Merriam-Webster's dictionary defines transformation as "a complete or major change in someone's or something's appearance, form, etc."[2] As you move forth in this journey, though your "bones" may be good and your earthly human structure may remain the same, the change that is awakened through conviction, brought face-to-face through confrontation, and enlightened through revelation will be constructed and finished through transformation. This only happens when you yield your mind, body, and spirit to God's direction and get a total "makeover" for your life.

If you are ready to change your patterns and behaviors, if you are ready to finish what you started, and if you are ready to move in excellence with passion and determination, then this book is for you! You are not alone on this journey. We are all in this together. As you hold this book right now, get ready—God is going to make you wholly *Fit for Your Assignment*.

SECTION ONE
ARE YOU FIT FOR YOUR ASSIGNMENT?

GOD'S CALLING OVER our lives is the assignment that we as children of God possess and are called to carry out. Every day presents new opportunities for us to embrace our call and assignment. There are too many people who spend a lifetime searching for personal fulfillment and never get there. That does not have to be your story.

Have you ever asked yourself, "What is my purpose in this vast universe?" It may seem like there are enough people to accomplish what needs to be accomplished. So there you sit, in the audience seat, watching a live show. You never know what comes next, but you watch eagerly as you fall into a trance of hopes and what ifs: "What if I could be that person I am watching? What if I could do what they are doing or have what they have?" The more you see, the more you question: "How did they get so blessed? Where does their confidence come from? How do they balance so many responsibilities?"

Well, I too had these questions. I would add that I often asked, "Lord, when is it going to be my turn? When will I see the blessings, the open doors, the hopes, dreams, and desires of my heart come to fruition?"

As time went by, I unintentionally drifted to life's sidelines and became a working spectator. I say "working" because I spent many years working arduously in ministry but not fully taking a hold of all God had for me. Fear, doubt, busyness, conformity, and procrastination all contributed to my sideline living—a state of mediocrity and personal neglect that ultimately led to my being unfit for God to perform His greater plan in my life! And He did have a greater plan.

The awesomeness of this truth is that He did not give up on me, just as He will never give up on you! When I surrendered to God's plan for my life and let go of the plans I had created for myself, I was set free. Faithful obedience and surrender to God's will made room for my gifts.

When you accept that all it takes is a genuine, "Yes, Lord, I will do, I will go, and I will be what You have declared for my life," doors of favor will begin to open.

Chapter 1

YOU HAVE AN ASSIGNMENT

[God,] who has saved us and [has] called us with a holy calling, not according to our works, but according to His own purpose and grace which was granted us in Christ Jesus from all eternity.

《 2 TIMOTHY 1:9, NAS 》

GOD HAS NOT called us to be spectators trapped in unfulfilled dreams, dwindled passion, and hopeless hunger for the greater things we feel are beyond our reach, nor does He want us to get comfortable in accepting mediocrity. God wants us to wake up every morning assured and aware of our purpose here on Earth.

If you do not know God's assignment for your life, then how do you suppose you will fulfill the call over your life? People who are certain of what they were called to do have passion, zeal, and a posture of determination. Despite the circumstances or unfavorable events of life, they press forward to complete their assignment.

You know you are on assignment when the assignment is so "shut up in your bones" that despite feelings of weariness, tiredness, frustration, and wanting to walk away, you can't because the assignment courses through every fiber of your entire being. Even if you wanted to quit and walk away, you couldn't because the passion and zeal have become part of your very existence.

If you have yet to discover your assignment, I encourage you to start right now by asking God to reveal His great purpose for your life. Do not spend another day, hour, or minute walking in mediocrity. It is not a coincidence that at this very moment you are holding this book. As a matter of fact, I am almost certain you have a longing and a desire to do more, be more, and to have more.

There comes a time when conformity ceases to exist. There also comes a time when we feel a desperate and overwhelming need to rise up and escape our caves of conformity.

I believe God has created alarm clocks inside each of us that awaken our spiritual senses. It is God's way of telling us, "Well, I waited for you. But since you can't wake up on your own, I will wake you and make you uncomfortable until you are walking in complete assurance, abundant joy, passion, and purpose." What a mighty God we serve! He does what He has to in order to get us to the place where we need to be.

Do not accept your current trials or circumstances as setbacks. Out of great chaos God provides the means for a new beginning.

Perhaps you are awakened by a thunderous noise that shakes the foundation of your home. You discover that the most valuable piece in the house has just been shattered beyond recognition. You tell yourself, "No matter what I do, it's impossible to pick up the pieces and restore. I will never be able to put this back together again." The decision is yours, my friend. You can stand in the midst of the broken pieces for hours, days, months, and years attempting to put it all back together and never see it return to its original form, or you can sweep up all the broken pieces and take them to the feet of Jesus. He will know what to do with them.

Similarly, when the storms of life shake our foundation and cause us to fall and shatter into pieces, in our brokenness we can confidently go before Jesus, the only person who knows exactly how to restore us to wholeness.

Sometimes in an effort to awaken us from our spiritual slumber, God allows valuable possessions to shatter. Strength, resilience, and dependence on God cannot be activated until there is a need.

Dependence on God requires such an active faith that as you surrender, though you may not know what the future holds—with the belief that God is in control—you are assured that all is well. When all is well, then you are introduced to your God-given purpose. Out of the rubble of pain and challenges you arise to discover and accomplish your greatest assignment.

It's Not All About You

When Jesus spoke to His disciples, He commissioned them to "go into all the world and preach the gospel to every creature" (Mark 16:15, NKJV). In essence Jesus wanted them to know that inside each of them was a message that others needed to hear. Let's look at three important principles in regard to this commission:

1. "Go." What He has given you, what He has deposited inside of you, is not to be kept in the confines of your own personal compartment. It must be shared with others.

2. "Into all the world." Yes, outside of you are people whom you have been called to serve: your family, community, a whole generation… You have been chosen to make a difference in someone's life. Perhaps the enemy has lied to you and told you in his most deceiving and convincing voice that you do not have purpose or that there are others in the trenches already, therefore your services and gifts are not needed. Well, I come against the lies in the name of Jesus as I declare over your life that you have indeed been chosen and destined for more. There is a unique gift and tailor-made assignment that is exclusively yours. There is someone out there waiting to see you, hear you, and know you. I invite you to receive it, believe it, embrace it, declare it, ignite it, stir it up, and walk in it.

3. "Preach the gospel." The Spirit of God is upon you. He has anointed, separated, and selected you to help meet

the needs of other human beings. Within you are expressions of encouragement, words of wisdom, and creative ideas. There are revelations to be revealed, a vision to behold, and a mission to fulfill. Someone needs to hear the good news that you, my friend, carry. Let loose and let go. Change your thinking and walk in your assignment, your anointing, and your gifting.

Every day you open your eyes, breathe a new breath, see the rising sun, hear the birds singing, feel the wind blowing, and hear the voices of your loved ones is simply an expression of God telling you, "You are here now and alive for purpose and great destiny." Moreover, it is God's way of revealing to you that the assignment over your life is not completed. Therefore a new day is introduced, providing a new opportunity to take hold of all that God has deposited inside of you. It is another opportunity to make a difference in someone's life.

You Have Been Set Apart

Did you know that before you were born, your assignment, purpose, and call were established? You were born for such a time as this. God has set you apart for the assignment over your life.

In the Scriptures the Lord tells Jeremiah, "Before I formed you in the womb I knew you, before you were born I set you apart; I appointed you as a prophet to the nations" (Jer. 1:5).

As we read this portion of Scripture, we witness a dialogue that takes place between the Lord and Jeremiah. The Lord revealed to Jeremiah that He knew him even before his very existence. The Lord formed and fashioned him. He set him apart and separated him to fulfill a great assignment. Jeremiah needed assurance of the Lord's providence over his life, and the Lord gave Jeremiah this assurance.

But then God delivers quite an impressive assignment (Jer. 1:5, 10). Jeremiah was assigned to speak to a sinful people and was called to bring conviction. Let's face it; this is not an easy assignment. I imagine Jeremiah felt unequipped for this particular assignment. We can see in verse 6 that Jeremiah did not embrace his assignment with great enthusiasm. As a matter of fact, Jeremiah resisted it.

He came up with a really good reason for why he did not believe he was the right man for the job. He told God he did not know how to speak (Jer. 1:6). Wait. Didn't God clearly make known that it was He who formed Jeremiah, knew him, and appointed him as a prophet? Yes, He did.

I am going to make a hypothesis as to why I believe Jeremiah said what he said. If I were in Jeremiah's predicament, the voice of fear would have drowned out the voice of God. In other words, the fear in me would have taken over to become the voice of reason.

Like Jeremiah, many of us to think we can pick and choose what assignment we are going to embrace—as if we have a choice.

Trust me, there were plenty of times when God clearly reminded me that He had already established and set me apart for a specific assignment. It was already written, declared, and established. I could not escape it even if I wanted to. I attempted every excuse I could think of. I even rationalized my excuses by trying to use God's inspired Word as justification. Ah, the things we do when we allow the voices of insecurity and inadequacy to take over.

Now, this is not always intentional. Sometimes it is difficult to accept God's great plan and purpose for our lives. His plan is so much greater than ours. It has unlimited possibilities. I mean, why would God trust you or me to execute an assignment with all our inabilities, shortcomings, insecurities, fears, and doubts? I'll tell you why: it is because God knows us better than we know ourselves. This means that whatever you think you are incapable of doing, God, by setting you up for a particular assignment, has already declared, "You can!" When you think you do not have the right words, know the right people, or have the right resources, let me remind you that "the one who calls you is faithful and he will do it" (1 Thess. 5:24).

A Glimpse of His Favor

At a very young age I knew there was something peculiar about me. I grew up in a Christian household. We attended church at least four times a week. The church I grew up in had a thriving children's program. Thursday evenings we had children's service. Children led worship, ministered in song, and even delivered sermons.

It wasn't until I was eleven years old that I was asked to sing a worship song. You see, I had been waiting for this moment. No one knew this, but one evening while at home, I began to sing. And for the first time my voice was unfamiliar to me. I realized I had a gift. I could sing; yes, I could sing!

Imagine, eleven years old and discovering a gift that was a kept secret until that very moment when God told everything around me to stop, to be silent, because He had something He wanted me to hear. He wanted me to hear the gift He had deposited inside of me. I remember saying to myself, "I can't wait till Thursday! I am going to sing!" But guess what? Thursday came around, and while I made my way to the front row, someone asked if I would sing. By the end of the song I experienced the warmth of people as they arose and glorified and worshipped God. I was not sure of what was happening, but I knew I had a gift that was greater than what I had initially realized. It went beyond singing; this gift provoked people to rise up and give God praise.

When God deposits something inside of us, it cannot be taken lightly. Whatever comes from God is bound to have an impact first on you and then on others around you. Something happened inside of me; there was a stirring that ignited in me a desire to discover God's plan for my life. Hence, the process had begun. I realize now that this was simply the beginning of the assignment and call over my life. I was given an assignment that would impact people and make room for God's favor over my and their lives. Through my voice people would be introduced to God. Whether through singing or through speaking, God had set me apart!

What if I told you I am an introvert? Yes, this girl right here stood on the altar for the very first time and sang with her eyes closed the entire ten minutes that felt more like ten hours! I was petrified, but I did not allow fear to stop me because I had just experienced a glimpse of God's favor.

You see, when God's assignment and purpose over your life enters the core of your very being, it pushes you into unknown dimensions. All of a sudden your dreams become larger than life, and you are open to a world of possibilities as you confront fear face-to-face and move boldly in your assignment. Despite your feelings of fear or insecurity, you are propelled to move forward. Your assignment becomes a lifestyle. You move in your assignment and live your life as a vessel used by God.

People Will Know You by Your Assignment

As a mother I know I am assigned to care for and nurture my two daughters. Motherhood is not the easiest of assignments. There have been moments where I have felt inadequate; I have been tested to the core, challenged in various areas of my life, and sought desperately to have the right answers. However, despite everything that comes my way, I am still my daughters' mother—this is my assignment! I cannot run from it. I could not deny it if I wanted to. Parenting is part of who I am. When my daughters introduce me to their friends, they begin their introductions with, "This is my mom." They affirm my assignment every time they call me mom.

As a pastor, working alongside my amazing husband, I am called to shepherd a flock—a *wonderful* flock, may I add—of amazing people. Assuming the role and responsibilities of the pastorate is also part of who I am. This too is my assignment.

Every time I am called mom, wife, and pastor, I am reminded of my assignment to serve others. I am also reminded of the responsibility I have to exercise self-care so that I can give the very best of me, so that I can give the very best of what God has deposited inside of me.

Truth is, we cannot give what we do not possess. We can try to "fake it until we make it," but I don't buy it. We cannot think we can fake being joyful and believe that we can give fake joy to someone else. This is why I stepped out of my comfort zone and took a leap of faith to pen the pages of this book. My goal is to shine a light or provide a beacon of hope—hope that will ignite you to understand that conformity, mediocrity, lack of passion, and maintaining the status quo just won't cut it. Because God has called you to so much more, something needs to change.

Discovery, activation, and revelation of your purpose, assignment, and call will not materialize until you recognize that without God it is impossible to successfully carry out the mission bestowed upon you. The truth is, dependency on God is necessary, if not crucial, to becoming a successful agent of change in the hands of God. You must understand that you are not self-sufficient but completely dependent on God. Everything must be aligned—your spirit, your thinking, your emotions, and yes, your physical body.

Spiritual Alignment Comes First

Have you heard the term *spiritual alignment*? I am sure you have. The *Free Dictionary* defines *alignment* as "the adjustment of parts in relation to each other";[1] for example, bringing forth to a straight line or an alliance where two parts come together arranged in the same form. Therefore, to be *spiritually* aligned is to be parallel with God as it pertains to His plan and purpose for your life; hence, your assignment. Let me warn you, this process can be painful. Try to straighten up completely erect after spending a long time bent over.

The Bible speaks of a woman who had this kind of experience in Luke chapter 13. This woman was bent over and could not straighten up for eighteen years. The Scripture says that a spirit caused her posture to be as such and afflicted her. Now imagine this woman looking down all the time, unable to straighten up. I imagine how difficult it must have been to wake up every morning misaligned, unable to stand erect. This woman must have endured great pain. Furthermore, the limitations endured and opportunities missed as a result of her condition perhaps caused emotional and psychological distress. This was not a good place to be. Yet many have made distress their dwelling place, as it feels ever present in their lives.

There are women and men who are living their lives crippled by spirits. Depression, anxiety, distress, fears, guilt, and regret, to name a few, have been carefully tucked under smiles, praises, eloquent words, and titles. *This is not God's plan for you! This is not God's plan for anyone!*

The enemy wants your spirit depleted of all that is good, of all that produces growth, peace, love, and passion. God wants you to live an abundant life.

When the darts of the enemy are launched toward your spirit with no mercy, they affect all aspects of your being. What you are dealing with is spiritual! If God is going to manifest His glory in your life, then spiritual alignment must take place. As you get in unison with God and seek to go to a deeper level, the depths and revelation of His Word get into the nooks and crannies of your soul, ridding you of everything that brings to a halt God's perfect plan for your life.

Remember my story of my being eleven years old and God starting me on a journey to discovering my assignment? Well, those were the days, my friend. I was walking in absolute bliss, happy to know I was special to God. Oh, what a feeling. My posture was upright as I affirmed vociferously, "I am sure of who I am." But the inevitable happened. I grew up. Seasons changed and life happened. I lost sight of the fact that I needed to nurture my spirit man. I got so engrossed in ministry that I forgot the minister in me needed care as well. In a nutshell, I had missed the mark.

My posture began to change so much that I could not see the greater plan for my future. I allowed all kinds of unhealthy things that may have seemed harmless at first to change my posture and knock me out of alignment. I was not in alignment with God. I got ahead of myself in some areas and fell behind in others. As a matter of fact, I might as well confess that a spirit of idleness came over me like a warm, cozy blanket. For a season I made sure I did not embrace *any* assignment that would keep me from my cozy blanket.

Let's face it; sometimes it just feels good to do absolutely nothing. I knew better, though. I knew this was not who God had created me to be. This was certainly not God's plan for my life, and let me reiterate, it is not God's plan for you either. The Bible clearly tells us that "the soul of the sluggard craves and gets nothing, while the soul of the diligent is richly supplied" (Prov. 13:4, ESV). The truth is, I avoided doing the work.

Funny how sometimes we want all the perks from heaven, yet we don't want to reach for heaven to get them. Spiritual alignment is going to require you to sit in God's presence and allow Him to cleanse you of all your impurities and toxins. You are going to have to pray until you are certain that you are aligned with God's purpose and will for your life. It does not always feel good. You will have to seek Him through Scripture, devotional time, and moments of silence. As a result you will begin to recognize His voice and understand His will and assignment for your life.

Being fit for your assignment requires that the work begin on the inside. For those who have been wounded, hurt, abused, mistreated, and abandoned, the mere thought of having to start here can be extremely overwhelming. Before I go on, let me encourage you, God has a greater purpose and plan for your life. There is more He wants to do in and through you. There are bigger dreams and higher dimensions to which He wants to take you. You must first look deep inside of *you* and bring out all that needs adjusting, aligning, ridding, molding, and cleansing. Don't be afraid. God is going to carry you through it. I know it can be difficult, but are you willing to risk watching your life pass by without ever discovering the greatness that resides inside of you?

I want you to know that I too wanted to run and hide the very moment I discovered the truth about myself. "What truth?" you ask. Well, where do I start? First, I discovered that God wanted to do much more, but I was the only one who was hindering and putting at risk all that God wanted to endow me with. I had placed limits and barriers, which I refused to remove. There were doors opening for me to speak beyond the East Coast, yet I allowed fear to set barricades that would keep me from walking onto an airplane and taking flight. Any event that required me to fly, I would ask my assistant to reject.

What was I doing? Did I really think I could close doors that God had opened? Yes, I did! But at that time I did what every good Christian with a conscience would do: I justified my bad behavior. I would say, "Lord, I know You understand me because You created me." Yes, I used grace and mercy to keep me covered. But if I told you that some of us take *advantage* of grace and mercy, would you agree with me?

It is so much easier to live in bliss, engrossed in some man-made definition of grace and mercy, than to live by biblical principles. These principles cause you to be governed by God's truths, which clearly shout out that transforming work begins with you. You must make a decision to accept the changes God wants to provide for your life. The Bible says, "Do not conform any longer to the pattern of this world, but be transformed by the renewing of your mind. Then you will be able to test and approve what God's will is—his good, pleasing and perfect will" (Rom. 12:2). Reality check: grace and mercy are available to all of us. However, we must gracefully and mercifully move into action by engaging in the process and task set before us.

We have to decide we are going to do whatever is necessary to partner with God as we move forward to becoming fit in all areas of our lives. We are not leaving any internal room untouched. We are going in and we are going to turn the light on, clean out the clutter, and rearrange the furniture in an effort to house the treasures, blessings, dreams, vision, purpose, and destiny God has for us.

The moment I decided I was going to embrace truth and set myself on a path to becoming fit for my assignment, I knew I had to be accountable to someone. It is not easy to let go of habits, faulty thinking, and all the other stuff that hinders our purpose. Who was I fooling? I had convinced myself for years that I was doing well, reaching and achieving all that I had set my mind to do. Yes, deep down inside my soul I knew that there was more. There had to be. I had wasted too many days regretting things I couldn't finish; hence my overeating, weariness, tiredness, overwhelming fears, and often feeling frustrated with myself.

Thinking back, it was hard to get up at times and face the fact that others were ahead of me, that others had greater discipline, more focus, better plans, and greater resources. Yes, sometimes while on assignment, rather than focusing on what is in front of us and moving toward it, we spend precious moments focused on those around us who are doing better, becoming greater, and achieving more. What a waste of my time that was! Goodness gracious, did I delay the process!

Well, I had made up my mind. I knew myself all too well. As a professional procrastinator and professional at sitting on the sidelines, I knew that at any moment I would stop what I had started and more than likely spend a good portion of my life *planning* to become fit rather than taking the steps toward activation.

God dealt with me about this, and consequently I created a secret group on Facebook where I began to post my journey. I was going to be accountable to somebody, or should I say, more than 750 somebodies, who later joined me on this journey. I invited women to my secret group (Fit for Your Assignment) and remained real, raw, and relevant, and off I went on my journey toward becoming wholly fit.

As someone once said, "I wish you a very good journey to an unknown you've never seen."[2]

A Post From the Fit for Your Assignment Facebook Group

God has shown me, through this group (Fit for Your Assignment), that my issues are deeply rooted in the past. He helped me to connect that it was not just about my body image but about my heart image, my mind image, and my God image. God mercifully woke me up to these realizations. I am on my way to being fit for my assignment.

⇒ *Reflections* ⇐

I am convinced there are three kinds of people:

1. Those who know their assignment and are living it out every day, walking in the fullness of joy, and reaping from all the seeds they have sown while on assignment.

2. Those who have yet to discover their assignment and have settled in conformity and routine. They work jobs that are unfulfilling, regret wrong decisions, feel guilty about not contributing, and lack meaning and purpose.

3. Those who know their assignment, yet their lives are such a mess that they spend their days overwhelmed with guilt, knowing they should be doing more but inhibited by all the chaos that surrounds them.

1. Of these three kinds of people, which do you think best describes you? Why?

_____

_____

_____

2. What has God awakened in you concerning this chapter?

_____

_____

_____

Chapter 2

YOUR BODY IS A TEMPLE

Don't you realize that your body is the temple of the Holy Spirit, who lives in you and was given to you by God? You do not belong to yourself, for God bought you with a high price. So you must honor God with your body.

« 1 CORINTHIANS 6:19–20, NLT »

LET ME START by saying that this journey is not about becoming skinny or achieving an ideal size or weight. It is about how a relationship with God, in conjunction with the Holy Spirit, is congruent with how we treat our body, mind, spirit, and soul.

If you recall, I started this book by going back to the day I looked at myself in the mirror and saw a girl who had deceived herself into thinking she was physically fit and in optimal health in all areas of her life. About the physically fit part, I am being kind. What I really meant to say is that I saw a girl who squeezed herself into an outfit that looked at least two sizes too small. This was a pivotal moment. It enabled me to grasp the seriousness of my situation. I had gained more than thirty pounds in a short period of time. Don't think for a second that I did not feel my unhealthy state of being. I sure did. I felt it every time I would get dressed, stand in a pulpit to speak, go up steps, and yes, with every *attempt* to exercise.

In fact, I was putting the assignment before me at risk of coming to a halt. I often felt tired, out of breath, frail, and unwilling to make any accommodations to promote better health. So I began to avoid anything that would cause my physical body to work harder than I felt it should. "I got this," I often told myself. The solution was simple: If I didn't want to feel out of breath, I would avoid exercise. If I wanted to feel skinny, I would buy a larger size and make sure that whatever piece of clothing I purchased was the miracle color—black.

In my opinion, black is the magic color to losing ten pounds instantly. It wasn't too long ago that my wardrobe consisted of all black colors. Wow, in hindsight I must have looked like I was going through the eternal mourning stage. It's really nice to walk into my closet today and see an array of pretty blues, greens, and tans. Yes, I did a pretty good job at camouflaging my neglect.

My Laundry List

As much as I tried to hide or convince myself that I was well and none of what I was doing was a sin, I knew something was wrong. The spirit man—the one who seeks a relationship with God—was silent and not actively engaged in the relationship. Although I knew God loved me unconditionally and that my worth was not based on a dress size, I knew I had taken over all areas where God was supposed to be the sole proprietor. What gave it away? Here is a list of things I experienced that indicated something had gone wrong:

- Uneasy spirit

- Working more and praying less

- Dependent on grace and mercy all the time and bypassing important principles

- Eating impulsively, not being mindful of what or where I was eating

- Lack of self-discipline

- Zero exercise—it wasn't in my vocabulary for more than two years

- Procrastinating—the "I will get to it tomorrow" syndrome

- Avoiding tasks that demanded more than I was willing to give at any particular moment

- Overwhelming fear of flying and of taking steps of faith

- Areas of my life were stagnate

- Not enough sleep

- Losing track of time, goals, and purpose

- Spiritually, emotionally, and physically drained

- Spending about two years not hearing from God on a personal level and not once inquiring of God about it (ouch, that one hurt)

- Feeling exploited and depleted

- Pouring out in ministry and not once stopping to fill up; ending up with an empty tank that took me nowhere for a season in time

Can you relate? I am not ashamed to share my laundry list of issues. I recognize there are far too many depleted, tired, and spiritually, emotionally, and physically drained men and women with great purpose—men and women with potential and destiny who are living in silence. These are people who are hiding in the torture chambers of pain, standing up in pulpits preaching a rich word yet feeling poor in spirit. Many are hiding in the confines of religion and man-made dogmas. And we wonder why we aren't seeing revival. *Personal* revival must come first if we are going to experience *corporate* revival.

The Utterance of a Desperate Soul

The enemy wants us to believe that if we come forward and confront our inadequacies, it will discredit who we are and the assignments over our lives. This is a lie that he uses to confine us to a life of regret and living below the standard God has set for us. Instead of going to God and asking Him to reveal the truth, many of us are afraid to make our request known unto God in prayer. We tend to view God as a merciless warden ready to punish rather than as a loving God ready to restore.

Anxiety, depression, fear, low self-esteem, regret, faulty thinking, and, yes, even our bad eating patterns all serve to affect our health, crush our spirit, and bring to a halt the assignment over our lives. The Bible says, "Be anxious for nothing, but in everything by prayer and supplication with thanksgiving let your requests be made known to God. And the peace of God, which surpasses all comprehension, will guard your hearts and your minds in Christ Jesus" (Phil. 4:6–7, NAS). The moment you open up to God to confess your personal struggles, something breaks in the atmosphere, and there is a release. It's as if God says, "OK, now it's My turn." He takes over.

There is something very powerful and liberating about releasing and surrendering to God all of who we are. Our spirit is alerted and our mind ignited into a different realm of hope and possibilities—a realm of change, purpose, presence, and worship. We are put in a posture of surrender so that God can cause the spiritual alignment needed to synchronize us with His plan for our lives. It is after we surrender that God can get to work without our senseless interruptions. Word of caution: God *will* go to the depths of your soul, and at times it may be very uncomfortable.

And the Walls Came Tumbling Down

Because I had a destiny and an assignment to fulfill, God moved my spirit man to a place of absolute discomfort. His voice felt thunderous deep within my soul, yet at the same time soothing with hope. His voice spoke with consistency until I surrendered to His invitation, which clearly stipulated, "Take a good look at yourself. Open the doors of those rooms you have kept tightly shut and allow Me to come in and do My greatest work."

Did you think this was really about the thirty pounds I had gained? Of course not. I want to take you deeper and beyond the obvious. I want to take you outside of what you can see with your naked eye. I want to take you into those areas that are not always apparent and obvious at first sight.

It is sometimes easier to avoid things that are not seen than to have to go into those hidden areas of our lives that house the culprit of our ailments and misalignment. I am speaking of those internal and unvisited places that thrive beneath titles, positions, roles, layers of clothing, and material things.

The truth is that in an effort to achieve total victory over problems and be successful in our assignment, the spirit, soul, and body must be dealt with in unison. Undoubtedly this was difficult for me. First I had to admit that I had internalized issues that needed to be brought forth and resolved.

"Seriously, God? I am good. We don't need to go there," I would often bemoan. But because God is not often moved by our fussing, kicking, and screaming, He went there.

Let me let you in on a personal confession. This is not easy, but here it goes. I have the kind of personality that doesn't like to display vulnerability. I have gone through my share of pain and struggles and have successfully hidden all of it in my own little private cave. I thought it a weakness to show anyone my pain, fears, and struggles. I mean, let's face it, I am a Christian woman called by God to minister to others. How dare I think I had the luxury to display my vulnerability—my humanity? I did not give myself permission to let others see my fragile soul. I built walls that I believed were vital if I was going to be respected, acknowledged, and validated as the person God had called me to be. I needed to let everyone know what a strong woman I was. The truth, however, is that this was a façade!

I allowed this demeanor to influence most areas of my life. I was determined to be the strong tower for everyone—friends, family, and ministry. Inevitably it backfired. As a result of my very own neatly built fortified city, the people around me did not dare stand at the gate, let alone make an attempt to go into the place where my vulnerable, human, emotional side resided. So in times of pain and distress I was left to my own devices.

Oh, I cried out to God during a difficult time in my life, "Please send someone to pray for me, to listen to me, to just ask me if I am OK."

I heard a voice speak back to me, "No one is coming. You have announced to everyone that you do not need people. Everyone thinks you are strong. You have all the answers to all of your problems. Isn't this what you pride yourself in?"

I responded, "No, I am not strong. Does anyone see my pain, my vulnerability, my struggles? I am human too! What have I done? Oh, God, what have I done?"

This harsh reality came in like a flood too strong for me to constrain.

But God

God knew me. God—my Creator, your Creator, our Creator— knew with much familiarity the troubles of my wounded soul. His unconditional love wrapped me, embraced me, loved me, and brought the walls of my very own city tumbling down. This temple needed searching. Better yet, it needed reconstruction.

I cried out like the psalmist, "O Lord, you have searched me and know me!" (Ps. 139:1). God knew the real me. Ah, yes, "deep calls unto deep" (Ps. 42:7, NKJV). The depths of my soul reached deep to the profoundness of God's infinite mercy. From the depths of my abyss the cry of a desperate soul penetrated through the confines of deceit, causing heaven to respond. The alleviating wisdom of God's Word, responded, "For when I am weak, then I am strong" (2 Cor. 12:10).

I realized I had a choice to make. Either I would allow the enemy to use my weaknesses to confine me to a tangled web of deceit, or I would allow God to be glorified in and through my weaknesses and turn what could have been into what would be. I chose the latter. I allowed God to rebuild the temple where the Holy Spirit could freely dwell. I was determined that this body was going to house the Holy Spirit, and anything that would hinder the Spirit from moving freely in my life had to go.

So you see, there aren't any shortcuts here. God deals intimately with us. When I say He wants to heal *all* areas of our lives, I mean all. God desires to take you to the point where there isn't anything left untouched—spirit, soul, or body.

Let's take this a step further.

Pneuma, Psyche, Soma

Scripture relates to the whole person as a living being—spirit, soul, and body.

> May God himself, the God of peace, sanctify you through and through. May your whole spirit, soul and body be kept blameless at the coming of our Lord Jesus Christ.
> —1 Thessalonians 5:23

The spirit, soul, and body all work intricately together. Let me set a foundation as it pertains to the spirit, soul, and body. It is imperative to understand their functions so that we can see the correlation and interaction among all three.

Spirit

- ◆ Greek word *pneuma*
- ◆ Characteristics of a human being that are spiritual

- Seeks a relationship with God as well as other spiritual beings

Soul

- Greek word *psyche*

- Involves the social and psychological aspects

- Involves the will, emotion, and mind

Body

- Greek word *soma*

- Pertains to the physical aspect of a human being

- Involves the senses: feeling, smelling, hearing, seeing, and tasting

Dr. R. E. Hawkins developed what he refers to as concentric circles to describe the forces that make up the self, in essence our personality. I was introduced to this model while working on my master's degree in professional counseling. I was immediately captivated by the spiritual implications this particular model has on a human being.

Among the circles stands the innermost circle, which is where the human spirit resides, acknowledging that we have been made in the image of God and, as such, possess a spirit. The spirit in each of us longs to fellowship with God. The Holy Spirit also resides in this circle, and therefore God is at the center (or core) of man's existence.

When fellowship is broken through sin, neglect, or disobedience, a battle begins within one's flesh, causing chaos to the inner man (or core).[1]

The reality is, this can happen to any of us. We don't wake up one day and tell ourselves that we are going to neglect our bodies. We don't tell ourselves that we are going to sin, disobey, and feel miserable. Of course not! What happens to us is gradual. It starts as a small act or thought.

For example, I would go out to restaurants with friends and treat myself to "comfort" food. (When it's all said and done, you experience everything but comfort.) The problem was not the comfort food I chose; I was the problem. I treated myself to comfort food one too many times. And when I came to my senses, I realized I had lost all sense of self-control as it pertained to my eating. The more I ate, the more I wanted. My flesh was celebrated. I indulged in my own weaknesses. Scripture says, "A man without self-control is like a city broken into and left without walls" (Prov. 25:28, RSV). The discipline of eating healthy ceased to exist. The truth is, it felt *really* good to eat, and oh, so comforting.

One of the greatest battles we as human beings face is the constant battle with the flesh. The remedy for victory over this battle is found in Galatians 5:16–17: "But I say, walk by the Spirit, and you won't fulfill the lust of the flesh. For the flesh lusts against the Spirit, and the Spirit against the flesh; and these are contrary to one another, that you may not do the things you desire" (WEB).

When I started the secret group Fit for Your Assignment, I was surprised at the number of women who immediately began to post their struggles about eating and lack of discipline. These women candidly spoke of their desires to fulfill their destiny and purpose while here on Earth. However, they didn't know where to begin or how to embark on a journey to win their battles. I knew almost immediately that God had placed something bigger than me in my hands. How amazing is God that He will take what could potentially destroy us—faulty thinking, bad eating habits, and the inability to recognize the importance of caring for our temple—and use it for kingdom purposes! In acknowledging the need we have for a God intervention in these areas, doors begin to open for God to manifest His glory in our lives.

From the onset I made it known that the vision of Fit for Your Assignment was more than becoming fit physically. It was more than exercise and more than a diet plan, but it would begin with spiritual fitness: "Spend your time and energy in training yourself for spiritual fitness. Physical exercise has some value, but spiritual exercise is much more important, for it promises a reward in both this life and the next. This is true, and everyone should accept it" (1 Tim. 4:7–9, NLT 1996).

There are many who have neglected their bodies, their hearts, their minds, and their relationships with God. This is not only applicable to women but to men as well.

Success

It is not hard to get off course in a fallen world. Just like the Nike slogan "Just Do It" implies, here stands a culture without boundaries or limits. The problem is that God's Word is clear in establishing that we do not belong to ourselves, for we have been purchased at a price (1 Cor. 6:19–20). Therefore we have an obligation to honor God with our bodies. Our temple has a purpose. God resides in our temple. His residence in our body ensures a prosperous life. I don't know of anyone who does not want to live a prosperous life. With regards to prosperity, I am not limiting its definition solely to material requisitions. I am speaking of prosperity of mind, body, and spirit.

Successful people will produce success in all area of their lives. A prosperous person is a person who has favor. To have favor from God is to succeed in all you do. Joseph had an assignment, and because he had favor from God, all he did prospered in his hands. Why? Because the Lord was with him and ensured that all Joseph did prospered.

Being fit for our assignment is about ensuring that whatever gift, talent, dream, vision, task, and assignment we have will attain its utmost potential. More importantly, being fit for your assignment ensures that all you do honors the God you serve—the God who resides in you. Therefore, in caring for your body, you are setting boundaries and establishing order. You are ensuring that the temple is clean and free of clutter and all the old debris from the past. It means you have self-control of what you feed your soul, spirit, and body.

You Can't Give What You Do Not Possess

Some time ago I was having a conversation with a wonderful young lady. She began to share with me some of the limitations she had that were primarily due to health issues. I asked her if she felt she had the power to change her circumstances. To my surprise she said yes. However, what she later said was more surprising. She told me that she knew she could change some things in her life that would help make her better and remove some of her limitations. She felt, however, that God loved her regardless of any limited abilities. She said she was a happy person just the way she was, despite her circumstances. She took a few steps closer to me and said, "Frankly, I don't want to change. I am comfortable the way I am. This has nothing to do with my salvation, so I am OK despite the condition of my health."

While I believed that she was a happy person and certainly agreed that God loved her, I couldn't walk away without letting her know that God wanted to give her so much more.

This woman is one of the most beautiful, talented worshippers I have had the pleasure of meeting. However, she was severely overweight and had self-imposed limitations as a consequence. I asked her if she knew what her assignment was. She paused, then looked at me and smiled shyly as if a bit unsure.

As her pastor and mentor, I asked if she was willing to embark on a journey that I believed would bring more greatness to her life. Without hesitation she smiled willingly and agreed to take my invitation, even before she knew what I would present her with. I told her I wanted her to discover her purpose in life.

Her demeanor changed. She hesitated. Her smile momentarily disappeared as she looked at me intensely without uttering a word.

I proceeded to expound on the challenge, telling her that I wanted her to spend time in prayer and ask God to reveal her assignment to her while she is still here on Earth. "When God reveals it, come back and see me," I said.

It wasn't long before she was back in my office with an answer. God had revealed her assignment.

She discovered that as a child of God she had dreams about her assignment. However, life happened. As a result she forgot about her dreams and passions and proceeded to live a life of complacency. She had decided to live the life that her environment and circumstances had produced. She had forgotten about the things she loved. But everything was about to change.

Now she knew her assignment and suddenly did not want to be held back anymore. She was ready to make the necessary changes that would prepare her to walk in her assignment. I told her it was not going to be an easy process but certainly a worthwhile one. Through counseling, prayer, and discipline this young lady embarked on becoming fit for her assignment.

I have seen the changes in her. But what I have been most impressed by is the conviction and awareness she possesses as she embraces each day. She confessed that she had mistreated and neglected her body. She discovered that her soul had been deprived of love from her family. She had been betrayed and abused. As a result, she chose to use food to fill a void that only God could fill.

There are so many similar stories of individuals with temples that are housing pain, betrayal, bad habits, and emotional trauma. Listen closely. God wants to change all this. God wants His children wholly fit. There is so much more that God wants to do. I am convinced that God is stirring the hearts of people. This may very well be you. There is more, much more. Do not limit God. Your body is an instrument God wants to use. The time for your breakthrough is now.

Take time to implement these simple yet profound measures that will get you on your way to being fit for your assignment:

- Pray—Be real with God. Tell Him everything, because you can. He loves you unconditionally. Let go. Pour yourself out in His presence.

- Read God's Word, the Holy Bible—Allow the Word to provide the revelation for this season in your life.

- Listen—Sit in silence. Allow God to minister to your spirit man.

- Invite Him—Invite Him to dwell inside of you. Call on the Holy Spirit and open the door to all those rooms you've held tightly shut. Let Him turn the light on and expose all things. He will carry you through.

OK, are we in the temple now? Are the lights on? Can you clearly see some of those things that have grieved the Holy Spirit, those things that have caused you to lose passion and zeal for life, those things that have held your assignment dormant? Great; now let's get to the heart of the matter.

A Post From the Fit for Your Assignment Facebook Group

 I had a week of emotional eating. But praise God I didn't gain a pound back. God is teaching me so much through this process. I've come to comprehend that getting fit for my assignment hasn't been an easy task, because my assignment isn't easy either. I can't treat this like any old thing. This is precious to God therefore precious to me. He is molding me, sanctifying me, and processing me for the assignment ahead.

⇒ *Reflections* ⇐

The spirit, soul, and body have an immense influence upon each other.

1. Your body is a temple of the Holy Spirit; how do you think you have neglected your temple?

_____

_____

_____

_____

_____

_____

2. What aspects of this chapter can you relate to and why?

_____

_____

_____

_____

_____

_____

Chapter 3

GETTING TO THE HEART OF THE MATTER

Guard your heart above all else, for it determines the course of your life.

« PROVERBS 4:23, NLT »

ANY YEARS AGO I was counseling a young lady who was barely fifteen and struggling with some deep-rooted issues. Moreover, she was being pulled in the wrong direction and influenced by the wrong environment. Temptation was everywhere. She found herself in a spiritual battle, ready to succumb to her flesh. She knew the Word of God, yet she was in a tug of war between the truth she knew and what she felt at the seat of her emotions—her heart.

I listened as she told me that someone she trusted and loved advised her to follow her heart. I knew all too well that my role was not to judge her. I was not there to discredit someone else's advice. Furthermore, if she was going to heed her friend's advice, I could only pray that the heart of this young lady was healthy and aligned with God's Word.

Although I was getting the impression she had made up her mind to follow her heart, I took the opportunity to provide her with a portion of Scripture I considered appropriate: Jeremiah 17:9, "The heart is deceitful above all things and beyond cure. Who can understand it?" When our session was over, we prayed together and said our farewells.

One month after our conversation she returned to my office. This time she came with a shattered heart. She said, "I followed my heart." She was hopeless, scared, depressed, angry, and ready to give up on life. As devastating as it was for me to hear the outcome of her decision, I knew that God was going to restore her.

Here is the good news: God is a God of second chances. God does not give up on us. Yes, there were detrimental consequences she had to confront, but God provided the strength. She rose out of the rubble of sin and dealt with the heart issues that virtually led to her demise. Today she is a beautiful married woman with a wonderful family and ministry. She is walking in her assignment because she turned her heart toward God.

So what is it about the heart that we need to understand? Let us begin by defining *heart* from a biblical and spiritual perspective.

Did you know that the Bible uses the word *heart* over nine hundred times? According to the *New International Bible Dictionary*, the *heart* is defined as

- The seat of affection

- The innermost being

- The center or core of one's spiritual and moral existence[1]

Our condition—who we are, what we think, and what we believe, including our emotions—stems from within the walls of our heart. The heart does matter, and if not carefully dealt with, it can potentially destroy us. When God begins to deal with us, He goes right to the heart—to the root of all issues.

So let me ask you, have you had your heart checked recently? I am referring to your spiritual heart, your spiritual pulse, and your spiritual heartbeat.

There is nothing wrong with going to the throne of God for well-visit checkups. You know, the kind of visit where you ask God to search your heart. Truth be told, I didn't do it as often as I should have. I found myself in a spiritual impasse. I was stuck and could not go any further.

Call 911. Please!

Wonder Woman

I truly believe that I was on the brink of a spiritual heart attack. I had all the symptoms. It started with a discomfort, an aching sensation. Something just did not feel right. But what was it? I loved being a mom and a wife. Pastoring a wonderful congregation alongside my husband was a delight (for the most part). I was receiving invitations to speak at conferences. It seemed as if God was doing wonderful things in my life. So what was I doing that made me feel this way?

The ache, discomfort, and restlessness would not go away. They progressively developed into spiritual pressure and tightness. Breathless and fatigued, I thought I could ignore the symptoms and all of the sensations would just dissipate. But no! The Holy Spirit was doing His job of convicting me that something was very wrong. Warning signs were everywhere, yet I did not see them.

Then one day God barricaded me in the privacy of my own home. He did not let me go any further. That day, when I looked at myself in the mirror and observed the reality before me, it all became clear. I had my response. Oh, I was on my assignment all right. However, I was not *fit* to successfully execute the assignment. As a matter of fact, I was like a train wreck waiting to happen.

I was trying extremely hard to be the best wife, mom, pastor, counselor, and student. For me trying hard meant go, go, go. Don't stop. Give it all you got. C'mon, Wonder Woman, you can do this!

And why not? I am a woman. I am strong. Really? No! Don't buy into that. Man or woman, it doesn't matter! Our dependence on God being the source of our strength is what makes all the difference. When we are weak, He is our strength. I needed this impressed into my spirit.

I Need You, Lord

If it is true that the heart is the hub or command center of our thoughts, belief systems, and appetites, as well as our spiritual and moral existence, then it was time for me to examine each carefully. I was not going to do this alone. I needed God. I needed God to search me and reveal to me the cause of my ailment and disarray. My prayer changed from "Give me! I want! Will You?" to "I need You, Lord. I need You now, tomorrow, and forever." My supplication was, "Change my heart, O Lord." I was praying without knowing which area of my heart was ill.

As I continued in prayer, something began to happen. All of my senses were awakened. I was exposed and truly ashamed. I remember one evening in particular; as I conjured up the courage for a self-analysis, I began to ask deep, internal questions: "Do you know why you do what you do? What is your motivation? Is it to please God or to build a name for yourself?" Wait! That last question—what was that all about? Seriously? What kind of question was that? Of course I do what I do because I want to please God! Wait. Did God want me to examine my motives? Of course He did.

As I searched the residence of my intentions, thankfully I discovered that I truly wanted to please God. There was a catch: I wanted to do it my way, at least for certain areas of my life. I was picking and choosing rather than totally surrendering! At times God will ask of us things that bring us face-to-face with our fears and inadequacies. God does not do this to torment us. Rather, He does it to free us. God wants us to live in the freedom that can only come from knowing Him and, via that conduit, know ourselves. In knowing Him we are reminded of our great assignment. We live to serve, worship, and honor Him in all we do.

Let's Do It My Way

I have a great passion for the Word of God. When I am able to relate God's Word and love to others, I feel a joy that is indescribable. However, not too long ago I suffered from aviatophobia—a fear of flying. So I made up my mind that if I received invitations that would require traveling by airplane, I would not take them. I would rather travel by car fifteen hours than get on an airplane. I had determined that I was never going to fly again. I had a horrible experience on a flight returning from a speaking engagement and had made up my mind—never again! I had placed limitations on the assignment because of my own fears.

The more I thought about flying, the more I feared it. Was this part of God's plan? Of course not. I had allowed fear to stagnate God's plan for my life. I went as far as telling God I was happy doing ministry from where I was. It was not necessary for Him to open any doors past the fifteen hours of travel distance by car, or anywhere else in this country or abroad that would require me to fly. I assured God that I would give it my all, but on my own terms.

Inside of me existed this spoiled, defiant three-year-old that insisted on getting her way. She was shouting, "It's going to be my way or no way!" This is what happens when we have spiritually impoverished compartments tucked away in our hearts.

Jesus looked at a crowd at one point in His ministry and said, "If anyone would come after me, he must deny himself and take up his cross and follow me" (Matt. 16:24). I needed an attitude adjustment. My actions were reflecting what my heart carried. I was carrying on as if God needed to do what I said. Behaviorally I was refusing to take up the cross. I wanted to follow God all the way, but about carrying the cross...Well, it depended how heavy it was.

We cannot falsely convince ourselves that God sits back and allows us to have it our way forever. At the end of the day God still reigns! I am reminded of when the people of Israel were begging for a king. They wanted to be like the nations around them. They could not see that they had been chosen for something different.

They had a king. God was their King. Through His prophet Samuel God was leading His people. Samuel began to take the people's demand quite personally. Samuel felt rejected, but the Lord assured him that this was not so much about Samuel as it was about Him—the Lord. The people had rejected the Lord as their King. In their hearts they had allowed other gods to rule. They had turned their eyes toward earthly desires.

The Lord informed Samuel that He would heed their requests and give them exactly what they asked for. But He said, "Warn them solemnly and let them know what the king who will reign over them will claim as his rights." (See 1 Samuel 8:9.) Do you think the people of Israel, upon hearing the warning, changed their minds? No! They did not. You see, their hearts were turned away from God. They looked outside of the eternal.

I had allowed fear to reign in my heart. Now it had claimed rights over my life. Fear readjusted the assignment over my life to accommodate itself and remain king. Whoever or whatever rules your heart reigns over your assignment.

I believe I am making my point clear. I was not doing well and was certainly unfit to continue on my assignment until there was spiritual renewal in my inner self.

In his book *Desiring God's Will* David Benner discusses two kingdoms: the kingdom of self and the kingdom of God.[2] He asserts that a person lives either in the kingdom of self or the kingdom of God. No one lives in both. One of the kingdoms has to be relinquished in order to obtain the other. The problem is that it is much easier to put your trust in what you believe you know rather than the One who knows you and has your future secured in the palms of His hands.

I was familiar with fear. When that airplane dropped thousands of feet in one instant, I had practically lost my breath. Vivid in my memory was the feeling of terror. I thought for certain the plane would fall out of the sky. I remember thinking, "I don't want to die like this." I remember the panicked expressions on the faces of other passengers as well as the silence of all the flight attendants on board. I thought, "I haven't fulfilled it all. Why would I go now?"

Well, I am still here, but fear also remained deeply imbedded in the fibers of my memory bank, and it planned on reigning for a while—a very long while. Fear became so great a force that for years it blocked my memory to all that had transpired.

You see, after about fifteen minutes of absolute panic, I picked up the Bible I had taken on board and desperately began to pray. I asked God to soothe my soul, to speak to me. He did. It was as if someone had turned the pages of my Bible to Proverbs 3:25–26 right before my very eyes. "Do not be afraid of sudden terror, nor of trouble from the wicked when it comes; for the LORD will be your confidence, and will keep your foot from being caught" (NKJV). At that moment my heart immediately aligned itself with the Word of God. The turbulence stopped, and the rest of the flight was as if the plane was traveling in the palms of God's hands and God Himself was carrying the plane to its destination.

So what happened? Why did I not get on board another airplane for almost six years? I fed my fear. I returned home and rather than speaking God's providence over my life, I was more interested in feeding the fear that had tried to overtake me. I fed it until it became greater than the miracle I had experienced.

For years, instead of speaking about the women's convention I had attended, the experience that had attempted to interrupt my assignment, and the miracle I had sustained, I spoke about the trauma and the fear that I was still allowing to plague my emotions. Yet God wanted to remind me that despite what came to attack me, I would be safe in His arms.

One of my husband's favorite sayings is, "If you feed it, it grows; if you starve it, it dies." I had starved the miracle and fed the fear. It held me captive for over six years. But no more. I had to make a decision. I finally decided that *I will* align myself with God. I decided that in all circumstances I would keep my heart toward God. I have a new fear now—the fear of the Lord.

This fear motivates me to seek Him every day and to keep His commandments.

Choose Wisely

A turnaround occurs when one is determined to turn one's heart toward God in total reliance and dependence. When this is entrenched in your spirit, it becomes evident in life's transactions. It also means that a decision must be made: which master will you serve? The Bible says, "No one can serve two masters" (Matt. 6:24). We all have to choose. Are we going to serve self, or are we going to serve God? I know one thing for sure, we cannot serve both.

I was behaving according to the condition of my heart, which was not as well as I thought it to be. It had been affected by personal experiences, losses, trials, tribulations, and betrayals. In addition, *self* wanted to reign alongside God. All of this resulted in a heart of disarray. I confess there were areas that were hardened as well. However, the plans of God are so extraordinary that He sends the Holy Spirit to stir us up, convict us, and awaken us to our harsh reality. He does this only to let us know His great plan for our lives. Our limited human capacity will never comprehend the depths of God's love for us.

Let me tell you some more.

About my eating habits... Well, let's just say this was one of the hardest areas of change I had to confront. For a season of my life I didn't see a problem; that is, until the Spirit of God put His finger on my eating issues. He showed me that my lack of control was taking a toll on my physical body, thus affecting my ability to move forward in my assignment. He helped me realize that if I did not do something, my lack of control was going to affect my ability to continue forth in God's purpose for my life.

How effective was I going to be if I was sick, tired, and unhealthy? Not only would I suffer, but so would my kids, husband, and everyone else I have been called to serve. This was bad stewardship on my part. I purposed that I would monitor my eating to see if I could get to the root of the problem.

After conducting my own personal experiment and documenting my eating patterns, I concluded I was a stress eater. This meant I ate more when I was under a lot of stress. The demands of the everyday routine, the demands of ministry responsibility, school, and life all contributed to my high levels of stress.

The Lord revealed it all. The Holy Spirit was actively engaged in my life. As I reflect on my journey, I am convinced that I did not have a choice. This is the way it was going to be. I belong to God, and my heart would not find rest until it was in the hands of its rightful owner.

The more I sought God, the more He revealed. I knew who was in charge now, and it wasn't me. My desires, passions, priorities, and appetites had changed. I longed for God more than ever. I was satisfied. I was at peace. My heart was at rest. In *Confessions* Saint Augustine writes, "You have made us for yourself, O Lord, and our heart is restless until it rests in you."[3]

I could hear God telling me, "I want you for Me." God wanted me to desire *Him* more than I desired anything else. I went in pursuit of God without any expectations. I stopped going to the throne of God with a list of "to dos" that would only benefit me. As a matter of fact, my prayer to God became more of "What can I do for You?" I let go of everything and surrendered my human volition.

As a therapist and minister, I have been invited into sacred, personal, and protected spaces. I have heard confessions and stories that have marked my life forever. I have come to respect those who have endured hardships that are beyond the scope of human comprehension. So when I speak of heart issues, I am mindful of the scars of abuse, addictions, betrayal, and losses that have hardened the hearts of many individuals. Notwithstanding, I have seen how the power of God's Word has transformed hearts that had been bleeding and left to die by the wayside. I have witnessed the resurrection of hearts that were spiritually dead. I have seen once-hopeless men and women cry out to God and experience life as if they had never lived before. I have witnessed what happens in that moment when the breath of God saturated the very core of their existence.

Sad to say, some people have grown accustomed to their state of being. For some, the peace of God has been replaced with anger and contention. For others, love has been replaced with hate, and forgiveness with unforgiveness. With each exchange the heart becomes increasingly ill.

The Echo of a Broken Spirit

On one occasion a lady came to my office to see me for counseling. I knew from the moment she walked in that she was distraught. After going through the preliminaries, I invited her to share with me the nature of her visit. As soon as she began to speak, I knew I was dealing with a hurt, angry woman who had been betrayed by her husband. She had been left with a child to raise by herself. This woman who sat before me had a broken spirit. Her internal state was evident in her physical manifestations. She was enraged. Her tone reflected the depth of her grief. She had a vindictive spirit and was determined to retaliate. Her pain was like fire consuming any sense of reasoning. She had bred so many negative emotions that she had become physically sick. She had neglected her spiritual life and had given herself over to earthly desires. She had given her heart solely and entirely to her husband and had neglected to care for her spiritual self. Her identity was entangled in the man she loved. When the walls came tumbling down, she had no spiritual defenses. She needed divine intervention.

Approximately thirty-five to forty minutes into our session, she paused. Silence filled the room. The presence of a force greater and more powerful than the echoes of her despair filled the room with hope and peace. It was evident God's presence was present. It was shattering every distorted fragment while providing an anesthetic to an agonizing soul.

After what seemed like an eternity (in reality about two to three minutes), she broke her silence with tears. She said, "This isn't really me. I am not a mean person. I am here because I need God."

Well, I could breathe a sigh of relief. Her words were music to my ears. We spoke a little more and prayed together.

When she walked out of my office, she walked out with her heart turned toward God. She surrendered to God that afternoon and placed all her cares at the feet of Jesus.

I do not know what happened to her afterward, but I do know what happened that day. A broken spirit was restored and despair turned to confidence. She left with a confidence that assured her she would make it as long as she clung to God. Yes, she would come out of the rubble of despair. Surrender is all it took to exchange mourning into dancing. She came in enraged but left empowered.

There is no other way but God's way if you are seeking to be fit in your heart. You may not have control of external influences. You may not be able to stop people from treating you a certain way. There may be some experiences you will simply have to face. You will have trials to endure and broken pieces to pick up. Your response, reaction, and willingness to do the right thing are what separate you from the rest.

This is not easy, but this is what the Lord showed me: First, you must determine in your heart that you will remain steadfast in Christ. This can only happen through a relationship with Him. It must be an intimate relationship, not a loose relationship. Your assignment and your path will remain on course when you acknowledge Him in all of your ways. When there is intimacy, there is a greater desire for more. You will find yourself wanting more of God, and in wanting more of God, you will want all that God has for you. More of God means less of you.

Next, you must relinquish all your plans and ideas that have stemmed from fleshly desires. You must surrender. Surrendering to God brought me the greatest peace. Once I surrendered, I didn't have to worry about producing my own outcome. God had my outcome in His hands.

I have decided not to question whatever God wants to do in my life. I will do whatever He asks of me. Worrying about having the proper resources or the right connections is irrelevant. As a matter of fact, my desires have completely changed. The things I thought were important have become less important.

I found out that when God started opening doors, all I had to do was surrender to God's plan, and He would supply all my needs. Surrender and obedience walk in tandem. They are interdependent. They cannot stand alone. My obedience to God destroyed my arrogance. Praise the Lord!

Arrogant people feel too important to apologize, admit their wrong, or take any responsibility for wrongdoing. God brought that tower down right from the very beginning of my process toward wholeness.

As I write, I find it hard to believe there was a time in my life I hid all these things in my heart. Talk about grace and mercy.

We tend to believe that because we hold titles and positions and have had opportunities to glimpse at God's favor over our lives, we can get away with bad behavior. Do you know how I got away with certain behaviors and evaded conviction? I justified my actions.

Allow me to give you the nontheological definition of *justification*: "A fact or circumstance that shows an action to be reasonable or necessary." Yes, this is pretty much how I operated. The more times I got away with it, the more I thought it was the right thing to do. I mean, let's face it; haven't we been taught to believe that titles provide us with the means to say whatever we want whenever we want?

How preposterous! If we are going to see change and experience both personal and corporate revival, we are going to have to change our thinking and our exchanges with other human beings. I had to surrender *completely* to God. Don't take the word *completely* casually. Completely is giving up all of you in totality and letting God solely reign. It is completely surrendering your behaviors, ideas, plans, and fears—all of them, until there is nothing left of you. Is it easy? No. But let me encourage you. Surrender may not be as hard as you may imagine, if you can trust God enough to let go.

"What is next, Reina?" you may ask. "I am willing to surrender. Come on. Bring it on. What is next?"

Here it is.

Take up your cross.

Are you ready to deny yourself for the sake of others? Are you ready to give up your interests for God's interests? Are you ready to bring a daily sacrifice to the altar of your soul and allow it to be consumed and rendered pleasing unto God?

Are you ready to starve those emotions and past issues that have kept you captive, trusting that God will take care of your business as you make it your business to take care of others?

Are you ready to exchange your fears for courage and walk into what is unknown—unknown to you but known to your Creator?

There is more.

At the moment of total exchange and surrender to God, your desire to know Him increases and a new relationship is birthed. A relationship with God will consist of worship as you move into a new realm naked and unashamed. You will feel safe in His presence. Prayer will be provoked as you desire to hear Him. Your soul will long to sit in His midst. This will be accomplished through prayer. You will understand that you are connected to a body, a community. You will feel a sense of belonging, worth, and value as you serve others. It will no longer be about pleasing "me" but about pleasing Him. You will acquire a sense of connectedness and social concern, which are indicative of spiritual and mental health.

When all your reliance is on God, no matter what comes your way, how difficult the storms, and how severe the pain, you will never, ever surrender to other gods. You will not surrender to internal rulers or outside influences. Nothing will separate you from the love of God!

Yanking the root of all issues from your heart makes room for

God to sow His Word, which will produce a man or woman after God's own heart. King David was not a perfect man. He had to confront and endure much. Yet he continued to move on to his assignment because he was a man after God's own heart. (See Acts 13:22.) His life of worship, devotion, and service provided the conviction necessary to confront his issues. He had a fear that drew him closer to God, not further away. He revered God. He knew to rise up and out of the waters that attempted to drown him. He was knocked down plenty of times but never taken out! His anchor was the Lord in whom he had placed his confidence. He suffered depression, anxiety, and pain, all because of his short-comings. Yet he knew where to turn his soul as he declared, "Why, my soul, are you downcast? Why so disturbed within me? Put your hope in God, for I will yet praise him, my Savior and my God" (Ps. 43:5, NIV).

Hear me. Let me impress this in your spirit. Know that when your heart is aligned with God, there is harmony. When you have proposed to guard your heart because you know that out of it flows life, there is no pain you cannot endure, no dream you cannot achieve, no battle you cannot win, and no assignment you cannot complete.

If your life matters, then your heart matters!

Can you relate to any of the following statements?

1. I am consumed with finding ways to make me happy.

2. I feel the need to prove my abilities and strengths to others.

3. I often think about those who have hurt me, and it makes me sad and/or angry.

4. I surrender to feelings and emotions that come at me with a fiery force—anger, contention, conflict...

5. I can't let go of the past, but it's OK. I can live with it. It doesn't affect me.

6. I don't need to spend time with God every day. He knows I love Him.

7. The simple pleasures of life make me most happy— material things such as cars, houses, earthly pleasures...

8. I will serve others after I serve myself. It's the right thing to do.

9. I am not consumed with having to do the right thing all the time. God knows I am human.

10. I have a greater desire to succeed than to surrender.

A Post From the Fit for Your Assignment Facebook Group

I just sometimes feel that all these blessings that I have received are still a dream...from a nobody to a somebody, just by me giving my heart to the Lord. My heart belongs to Him. Thank You, Jesus. I wouldn't have it any other way.

➡ *Reflections* ⬅

When God deals with us, He goes right to the heart.

1. Are there some heart issues you want to give to God and allow Him to deal with?

_____

_____

_____

_____

_____

_____

2. After reading this chapter, if you could write a letter to God, what would it say?

_____

_____

_____

_____

_____

_____

Chapter 4

IT'S ALL ABOUT CHOICES

Do not be deceived: God is not mocked, for whatever one sows, that will he also reap. For the one who sows to his own flesh will from the flesh reap corruption, but the one who sows to the Spirit will from the Spirit reap eternal life.

« GALATIANS 6:7–8, ESV »

EVERY DAY BEGINS with choices. From the very moment we wake up until the moment we end our day, we make choices. We choose what we wear, how we comb our hair, and what we eat. In life we choose the car we drive, the house we live in, and the people we decide to call our friends. We live in a society of choices—the right to choose and the power to choose an alternative. Variety is everywhere—colors, tastes, shapes, and brands. The list is endless. We are so accustomed to making choices that we make them on demand, oftentimes without giving them a second thought. What if I told you that the choices you make on a daily basis could accelerate you, delay you, bring you into the greatest place of your life, or send you spiraling into the lowest pit?

The culture we live in tells us that choices are a part of our rights. But wait. Have we forgotten that attached to those choices are consequences? For every choice we make there is a consequence. Every day we wake up to the consequences of the choices we have made throughout our life. For some people this is good news. For others it is a painful reality to face. I cannot help but think of the numerous people who have told me that if they had a chance to do some things over, they would make very different choices.

The choices you make in life should derive from the love you have for God, along with the desire to walk in obedience to Him. There should be a genuine desire to abstain from anything that would jeopardize the relationship you have with God.

I am reminded of a divorced woman I know who has endured disappointment after disappointment throughout the course of her life. I admire her spirit. She loves God with all her heart. She serves God and others unconditionally. After years of being alone, she met someone and embarked on a relationship. Throughout her relationship she continued to be faithful to God and the call over her life. She was careful not to grieve God with any actions that might hinder her assignment.

One day she approached me to share some concerns. After noticing some red flags, she felt as though she needed to reevaluate the future of this new relationship. There were discrepancies in the man's character she could not ignore. She was at a crossroads and had a choice to make. She could ignore what the spirit inside her was revealing and choose to follow the desires of her flesh, or she could walk away from the man she planned to spend the rest of her life with, trusting that the Holy Spirit was calling out to her, bringing conviction, and preventing a disaster from taking place. She decided to walk away from the relationship, trusting that God was directing her and had her best interest at heart. She understood that her future and her destiny would be as good or as bad as the choices she made.

Everyone should have a moral compass to help guide their decision-making process. For me it is the Word of God. The Word of God provides the instructions I need for conducting myself and living a life that is pleasing unto Him. The Word of God is a "lamp unto my feet" (Ps. 119:105, ASV). Everywhere I go and every decision I make, along with all of my convictions, are as a result of the active Word of God in my life. However, there was a season in my life when this was not the case.

Let me be transparent. I have talked about the thirty pounds I gained within a short period of time. I first discovered I had gained the weight when I went to the doctor for a routine checkup. I don't know about you, but I refuse to get on a scale until I first remove my shoes, earrings, coat, sweater, and anything else that may add weight. Quite frankly, scales scare me more than going to the dentist for a root canal—in particular, those digital scales that post your weight in 100-point font for the viewing pleasure of an entire office. Those scales terrify me. I could not believe my eyes. Surely this was a mistake. How could I have gained thirty pounds?

Apparently there were bigger issues with me than the mere change in appearance the extra weight had caused. There were potential health risks to consider. Did I really think I could get away with eating all those late-night meals and not pay the consequences? Did I think that my bad eating choices would not produce less-than-attractive results? Well, the truth is, I never took the time to ponder the extent of the possible consequences. What about the constant habit of eating out rather than enjoying a good, home-cooked meal, one where I could implement portion control and the ingredients that went into making them? My justification? I was too busy, and it was more feasible to have someone else do the cooking, right? No. Of course not. Had I taken the time to implement proper planning, I could have prepared healthy meals at home. The truth remained: I had no excuse.

Wait a minute. This was not just about me. I had dragged my family along with me. They too had been affected. I was driving a car full of passengers I loved into a junk-food wonderland. Moreover, I was neglecting my assignment as a mother. I was failing to provide sound guidance and healthy eating habits. I failed to have open discussions about how our bodies are the temples of the Holy Spirit. When did I stop believing this was important? There was a time when I was mindful about these things. Somewhere along the journey I lost sight of the greater plan God had for me and began to live only for the moment.

The Holy Spirit dealt with me. It was part of the alignment

process. God was not going to leave any stone unturned, and I welcomed it. You see, if we are going to move in the fullness of all God has for us, we cannot resist the process. It is imperative to understand that if we are going to live a life of purpose and truly live *on* purpose, we must be willing to let God prune us as a gardener prunes his prized rosebushes. Pruning removes all kinds of habits, malice, anger, bitterness, unforgiveness, and everything that stands in the way of our assignment. Pruning is necessary, as it brings healing to the spirit, soul, and body.

I concluded that whatever condition my spirit, soul, and body were in was a result of the choices I had made. I recognize that this may be difficult to admit, but when we make this type of acknowledgment, we take ownership of the fact that we are responsible for the condition we are in.

Taking responsibility means no one else is to blame. No one is to be blamed for the outcome except the person making the choices. *I* chose to eat junk food. *I* chose to do certain things my way rather than to depend on God's wisdom. *I* was reaping what I had sown. I felt terrible.

When conviction strikes at the heart, it awakens your spiritual senses. I knew that my eating was the result of a greater issue. I felt the weight of my choices upon me in more ways than one. I had sent conflicting messages to my daughters. I had not established boundaries. Now I had to decide whether to wallow in my consequences or get up and make the necessary changes. I chose to get up, and I did it without further delay.

Sometimes the best solution is to face the situation head-on instead of sitting in defeat pondering on the who, what, when, where, and how. I did four things right away that I think can help you, should you find yourself in a similar situation:

1. Get up

2. Crucify the flesh

3. Hold steadfast to God's Word

4. Keep moving

Get Up

Say to them, "This is what the LORD says: 'When people fall down, do they not get up? When someone turns away, do they not return?'"

—JEREMIAH 8:4, NIV

The enemy wants nothing more than to keep you bound in guilt and regret. If you remain in your present condition and allow the consequences of poor choices to dictate the rest of your life, you are never going to walk into the promises God has for you. We have all missed the mark at some point in our lives. Does this mean that the assignment over your life has been canceled and therefore you should surrender?

Should you really give up on having good relationships because one relationship failed?

Are you going to stop trusting people because there were people you allowed in your life who betrayed you?

Are you going to give up on yourself because you cannot imagine how you will recover from the decisions and the choices you have made?

Absolutely not! Don't you dare give up now. Instead, get up! Wipe your tears. Get yourself together. Keep your eyes on the vision ahead of you and trust that God is pointing you in the right direction. The only way to get up fast is to get down fast. Get down on your knees and ask God to set you back on the path He has chosen for you. God also made a choice when He chose you for your particular assignment. He created you, imparted greatness into you, placed His hand upon you, and anointed you. God set you apart for your assignment. He chose you out of all the people in this vast universe. You have been created for something so extraordinary and so specific, only you can execute it. John

15:16 says, "You did not choose Me but I chose you, and appointed you that you would go and bear fruit" (NAS).

I got down on my knees. I went to the Lord in prayer and supplication. I repented for all my wrong choices and for neglecting those specific areas of my life. Moreover, I repented for using food as a crutch rather than turning to Him for support and comfort. I wanted God to lead me every step of the way. I could not change my past, but I was going to change today so that my tomorrow would bear its fruit.

I looked at myself in the mirror and envisioned a sound mind, a healthy heart, and a determined woman of purpose. Every automatic thought that was not in alignment with the Word of God I rejected and did not allow it to make my heart its dwelling place. I was ready. I was determined.

No more sideline spectating

Our church was getting ready to do a Daniel fast, and for the first time in years I decided to join in. You read correctly. Prior to that I had come up with every excuse imaginable for why I could not be part of the fast. But this year was different. This time I had determined in my heart that anything that would draw me closer to God and align my life for great purpose, I would embrace.

Crucify the Flesh

> But I say, walk by the Spirit, and you will not gratify the desires of the flesh.
>
> —GALATIANS 5:16, ESV

Don't ever think for one second that you can negotiate with your flesh. The flesh is not submissive. It is never satisfied. The flesh is an enemy to the spirit man and always at war. The only way to stop the flesh is to crucify it, or it will crucify you. Everyone battles the flesh, including Christians. Alignment with God will determine the outcome in the battle between the spirit and the flesh.

As you walk in the spirit, your soul is nurtured and you begin to produce fruit.

Let me tell you how you know your spirit is aligned and your heart is turned toward God: the spirit stands strong at the gate of your temple watching and waiting. When fleshly desires and appetites arise, and they will arise, the spirit will rise up within you, and the war between the flesh and spirit begins. This is the good news.

When the Spirit of God is engaged, it is the job of the Spirit to keep those flesh-driven desires and appetites from entering your temple. The more you nurture your spirit, the stronger your spirit becomes, reducing the power the flesh has over you. The flesh says, "I can do whatever I want to do. It's my body." The spirit responds, "No, you cannot do whatever you want. Your body belongs to God. It is the temple where the Spirit dwells."

Crucifying the flesh meant I had to submit self. This does not happen overnight. There is a process. The more I said no to unhealthy eating choices, the easier it became. The habit of negating and submitting then became a part of my life. Today it is an automatic reaction.

Keep in mind that every time you give something up, you have to replace it with something else. And so I replaced unhealthy eating choices with better ones. I prayed. I researched and found alternatives. I decided I was going to try new things. I gave up fear and picked up courage.

The more I nurtured my spirit, the stronger I felt. I was awakened to a reality: the enemy never rests, so why should I? I do not mean rest in the physical sense—as you already know I promote self-care—but rather the alertness of the spirit within always watching out for the schemes of the enemy. I have made a conscious decision. I have chosen to seek Him daily through time of personal devotion, meditation, and worship. I learned how to use the spiritual gift of discernment to help me navigate through those times when I reach an impasse. These choices assure me that in the battle between the flesh and the spirit my alignment with God will determine the victor. I was not going to let God down. He trusted me with something, and I was going to ensure that I was fit to meet His expectations. So if change is what He asked of me, then change is what I was going to do.

Stand on the Word

For the word of God is living and active.
—Hebrews 4:12, esv

Let me keep it simple. The Word of God is life!

Do you want to live to the fullest? Do you want to see the promises over your life come to pass? Then stand on the Word that is alive inside of you. I realized I had a lot of Word inside me I had not been activating. I was ready to take the Word of God and make it mine. If I declared I was more than a conqueror, then I was more than a conqueror. I recognized I had to first believe the Word for myself before I could share it with others. Not only was I going to believe it, but I was also going to take it a step further and activate it. I was going to stir it up in my soul so that I would be ready to share it with others. I spoke life into those areas that had become stagnant and dormant. A relationship began between the Word and me unlike anything I had ever experienced before.

As someone who has been called to minister the Word, I would prepare sermons that God used to touch others. However, as I surrendered to God, He showed me that He had a particular word for *me*—a word that would touch me on a daily basis. What a wonderful God!

God wants us to serve others, but He also wants us to care of ourselves—and, I dare say, take care of ourselves *first*. By this I do not mean it's OK to be egocentric and selfish. I simply mean self-care, personal nurturing, a daily healthy dosage of God-calories. God understands that we cannot give what we ourselves do not possess.

Keep It Moving

The LORD said to Moses, "Why do you cry out to me? Tell the Israelites to go forward. But you lift up your staff, and stretch out your hand over the sea and divide it, that the Israelites may go into the sea on dry ground."
—EXODUS 14:15–16, NRSV

This is exactly what is expected of us when we are confronted with setbacks. Don't you know that your setback is a setup for a comeback? The people of Israel saw the impossible before them. Let's be real. I know that if I was encountering the unpredictability of the Red Sea before me and a band of hungry-for-flesh enemies behind me, I too would worry! Wouldn't you?

God takes the Israelites out of Egypt, and now they are faced with a huge obstacle. The enemies—which, by the way, God has delivered His people from already—are right at their heels. They knew they had to move forward, but the Red Sea was right in front of them. No wonder Moses was crying out to God, but God responded by asking Moses why he was crying.

I wonder what God meant by that. My response to God would have been, "Are You kidding, Lord? Why am I crying out to You? This was *Your* idea. This is the assignment You gave me. Now I have all these antagonists pursuing me, and I don't know what to do!"

Would you consider the possibility that God was saying, "OK, Moses. You can sit there and cry as the enemy gets closer, or you can get up and use your tools and the power I've placed in your hands. Did I not tell you that I would perform miracles with your staff? Let's go, Moses. You have everything you need to get out of this mess. Keep it moving! You are not finished with your assignment."

That is just what I did. I decided to keep it moving.

I used the power that prayer and the Word of God provided me, and I moved forward. I had to choose whether to end the assignment as I listened to the enemy tell me, "You don't have what it takes," or I could get up and move in the unknown. I could move with the One who knew exactly where I was meant to go. I made my choice. I moved forward in power and authority, and I have never looked back.

You can do the same. Get up! Take a hold of the power and authority God has given you and keep on moving. Your God-given assignment is waiting.

Let me take a moment to credit my heart issues for the way things played out in my life for a season. I would have never thought I would find myself examining my life in such depth.

Throughout my life I have inclined myself to being more mindful of the big choices and decisions I had to make rather than the everyday choices. When I was a teenager, I chose to pray about the man who would be my husband. Today I have an amazing man by my side—a man after God's own heart. I prayed about the calling over my life and that when doors opened for me, I would be able to choose which ones to walk through. I prayed about the big life decisions, but here is where I was an epic failure: I did not think there was a choice in how I would go about my day-to-day.

If I woke up in a bad mood, my response would be, "It is what it is." I could have chosen to take my moody, grumpy, self-centered self to the throne of God and bring it under submission. But no! I did not think it was necessary to spend my morning submerging myself in God's presence about my attitude when there were so many more important things to do and talk to God about. Besides, my prayer time was not in the morning. It was in the evening. Ouch, did I just share that? My morning prayers were quick. My evening prayers were more in-depth. Maybe I was the only person with this distorted mind-set. Thank God I have been set free from such distortion.

What I neglected to understand was that on those days when I decided I was not in the mood to interact with people, there might have been a wounded soul who needed a word of encouragement from me. I may have missed an opportunity to demonstrate God's love because I chose not to do anything about my mood. How many God-moments did I miss because I was so consumed with the "big picture" that I failed to see the opportunities God was presenting me on a daily basis? Let's take a praise break while I thank God for deliverance and a new way of serving Him! Thank You, God, for a change of heart.

You have choices to make. Daily choices. Yes, God has an enormous picture designed for your life, but like a beautifully designed mosaic, the big picture is a composition of daily choices. Don't leave anything to chance. God wants to hear from you despite how insignificant you think your issue or request may be. Learn from my mistakes and begin now. God is waiting!

Before moving into the next chapter, let me leave you with this: To smile is a choice. To change is a choice. To start over is a choice. To have a positive attitude is a choice. To live in victory rather than in misery is a choice. To embrace the assignment over your life is a choice. To choose is a choice in itself. Whenever you find yourself in a place where you need to make a choice, ask yourself, will your choice exalt *your* name or the name of God? After all, God made a choice. He chose to love you, save you, and trust you with an assignment.

A Post From the Fit for Your Assignment Facebook Group

Pastor Reina, your words have touched me deeply. They brought so much conviction that I knew I had to make a decision once and for all. My marriage was falling apart, my mind was going crazy, and I was depressed and disgusted with myself. I can tell you this today: I am not where I used to be. God has it all under control. God is doing amazing things.

⇒ *Reflections* ⇐

The choices you make today either accelerate or delay your assignment.

1. Can you think of a choice you made that either accelerated you or delayed you while on assignment? What was it?

---

2. Write a letter to self. Go ahead; be honest.

Chapter 5

CHANGE FROM THE INSIDE OUT

So here's what I want you to do, God helping you: Take
your everyday, ordinary life—your sleeping, eating,
going-to-work, and walking-around-life—and place
it before God as an offering. Embracing what God
does for you is the best thing you can do for him.
Don't become so well-adjusted to your culture that
you fit into it without even thinking. Instead, fix your
attention on God. You'll be changed from the inside
out. Readily recognize what he wants from you, and
quickly respond to it. Unlike the culture around you,
always dragging you down to its level of immaturity,
God brings the best out of you, develops well-formed
maturity in you.

« ROMANS 12:1–2, THE MESSAGE »

I INVITE YOU TO ponder for a moment. When was the last
time you looked deep inside your soul, and after soul-gazing
you said, "I am one beautiful soul"? Or maybe you have done
the opposite. You avoided bringing your soul to the mirror, where
truth and honesty reign, afraid that it would reveal the true condition of your heart. As strange as this may seem, it would do all
of us some good to carve out time to walk those areas of our lives
that may not be visible physically but are clearly evident in our
everyday walk.

Did you know God wants you to live the kind of life that will cause you to walk into His presence naked and unashamed? A place where, despite the circumstances and challenges surrounding you, you can declare, "It is well with my soul"?

The moment you understand that it is well with your soul, you will be able to acknowledge that "all" is well regardless of what things may seem like. That is the plan of God, that you may possess the ability to wake up every day and declare victory over your life. You can do this when you are well aware of the One who gives you peace, hope, and causes you to prosper. God wants you to live a life that no matter how big or impossible you believe your assignment to be, you will not be overwhelmed by it because you understand that your God is bigger. This can only come as a result of a soul that is aligned with God.

Extreme Makeover

Welcome to a culture obsessed with physical appearances. According to an article written in the *Huffington Post*, in 2011 approximately $10.4 billion had been spent on cosmetic surgery alone. In 2012 it grew to over $11 billion. Botox, liposuction, breast augmentation, and eyelid surgery were among the top surgical procedures.[1]

With the amount of money being spent on appearance, you would think that this would translate to a happier and more satisfied society. However, a recent study in *Psychology Today* found that even though most people who have plastic surgery are happy with the outcome, there were no significant changes in symptoms of depression or self-esteem.[2]

I do not bring this up to discuss whether cosmetic surgery is right or wrong; I respectfully submit that this is not the intent. What I do want to point out is that these studies prove that no matter how much we do to our outside, if our inside isn't whole, we will not find true joy, happiness, value, or fulfillment.

Of course, I believe that we should care for our outer appearance, and part of our assignment is to promote good stewardship as it pertains to how we present ourselves to others. Notwithstanding, our worth and intrinsic value must come from within. Hence, if we are made in the image of God, then our value stems from His image.

We have a body. We have a soul. We have a spirit. If we are going to see wholeness in all areas of our lives, we need to allow God to take the scalpel and begin to chisel away at our soul. Those who have an assignment attract people not by their appearance, but by the beauty of their soul.

I heard a story at a women's conference several years ago. The guest speaker for the evening shared that when she was ready to marry her husband, she asked him what he thought was most attractive about her. He responded, "I fell in love with your soul." He was able to see beyond the physical aspects of his soon-to-be bride because the inward man (woman) was evident in her everyday living. What does this mean? It means that as you move on your assignment, your emotions are balanced, thoughts are aligned, and values are firmly in place. These are all evident, not just on the good days, but every day.

The Lord showed me that no diet plan existed that would rid me of my thirty pounds. (Remember those?) God made known to me that unless I got rid of the junk in my soul, no matter how much weight I managed to lose, I would never be truly healthy. As a matter of fact, without the proper attention to my soul, it would simply be a matter of time before I would find myself in the same predicament. I knew it was time to go into some areas that, up to that point, had been untouched and thoroughly neglected.

Living in a Cocoon

Let me share some things with you that, although very personal to me, are relevant to share with you. For a season in my life I thought there were certain things I had to tolerate, things I had to surrender to. I thought this was part of my assignment in ministry.

For example, I was enslaved to a certain frame of mind. I

convinced myself to accept as truth that as a minister, I was not allowed to share my feelings with anyone. I told myself I was not allowed to have too many friends. If I hurt, I had to get over it very quickly because a congregation depended on me. If people offended me, I had to brush it off and walk away.

I spent many years in this mode of thinking. I became an extremist—a minister without balance, isolated in my own religious cocoon. As a result, I accumulated a lot of junk in my soul. My heart was hardening. During times of trials, people would ask me if I was OK, and I would smile and say, "Yes, I am fine. As a matter of fact, I am great." I really did think I was OK. I thought I was strong enough to take all the darts hitting my soul. I really thought my ability to endure pain was one of the reasons God trusted me with my assignment. At least, this is what I had convinced myself to believe.

Does this sound like a self-righteous kind of spirit? Or was I in absolute denial? I would venture to say it was both. You see, I was not being transformed. My mind was not being renewed every day. I had conformed to a mode of thinking, accepting that some of these hurtful things were part of my fate and, thus, permissible.

That is what we do, do we not? We conform. It is so much easier to simply go with the flow and wait patiently for everything to work itself out. This does not require a lot of work, now does it? But for those of us who know beyond a shadow of a doubt that there is more life to live and that we are in active pursuit of it, conformity is not an option. Transformation then becomes non-negotiable. Transformation is a critical component to becoming fit for your assignment. I will talk in more detail about transformation in a later chapter.

What did I discover? I discovered that my soul was affected by false religious and dogmatic garbage that I was responsible for fashioning. Many times I would become bitter and could not explain why. Why would I get sporadic visitations of bitterness? I had developed destructive patterns that would plague me, and destructive patterns are assignment killers. I praise God that He came on time!

Did I forget to mention that we could fail and continue to get it twisted and wrong, but God still has a way of bringing us back to the place of absolute purpose and destiny? Do not think for a moment that God will let you get away with ongoing inadequacies. It is in our brokenness that He becomes intimate with us.

This Is War

All I had to say was, "God, I hear You knocking. Please come right in." He stirred up the spirit man in me. The spirit pulled on the soul, the soul surrendered, and the body reacted. Did you get that? Your body may very well be reacting to the affliction of the soul, provoked by the influence of spirit—good or bad.

The mind-set of Christ and my mind-set came head-to-head. All along I thought I had the mind-set of Christ. For a moment I thought, "God, why are You fighting me? Aren't we on the same page?" I could not understand.

It wasn't until I became sensitive to the voice of God speaking to my thoughts, my emotions, and my desires that I began to see with clarity. I could hear the sweet voice of God. I really cannot explain it. I just knew it was Him. With every word that penetrated my heart, His voice soothed my soul. Like a double-edged sword, it pierced through everything I thought was right. Time stopped. His presence engulfed my very existence as He lifted my head and began to embrace me with His truth.

His truth declared that it was OK to feel downcast. It was OK to ask for prayer. It was OK to look at someone and say, "You've hurt me." It was OK to be *me* and still remain on my assignment. God had just given me permission to be human. God never asked me to take on His role. He simply wanted me to acknowledge Him in all my ways.

There was a new me, and I was ready to move in my assignment. I became real, raw, and relevant. My spirit felt alive again. I felt free! I could feel! I could cry! I could share with others that this journey was all part of my assignment.

How about you? Are you ready to live in utmost freedom? Are you ready to be released from the bondage of people-pleasing, guilt-swallowing hopelessness? You were created to be *you*. No one can be a better you than you! It's time! It's time to let your emotions known. It's time to come out of your shell and feel alive! It's time to cry yet not feel like you are drowning in a bottomless pit of hopelessness, because you know that One greater than you has you in the palm of His hand. It's time to rise up and execute your assignment.

Now, keep in mind, there are boundaries to be exercised in this area. Wisdom ought to be executed, particularly when dealing with personal matters of your life. Your character and integrity are important.

Using godly wisdom, I began to share with others about my own shortcomings and shared some particular struggles as circumstances allowed. The more I spoke to people, the more freedom I felt. Women and men began sharing their struggles with me and would eagerly ask me for prayer. I began to see the extent of the impact I was having when after each speaking engagement, people would approach me and say, "Thank you for sharing. There is hope for me."

When I refer to the word *raw*, I mean unadulterated. I was speaking the unadulterated, clean, and pure Word of God. I began to minister the Word of God with a newfound passion. I became real, sincere, and authentic. This does not mean I had not been sincere before, but now I was ministering with transparency. It stemmed from God's heart flowing through me. It did not stem from my own shortcomings and unstable mind-set. I was free to be me.

Sometimes we think our relationship with God is perfectly aligned to God's purpose. Nonetheless, our hearts are far from God. I learned that one way to measure whether the heart is aligned with God is to check and see if there is an everyday pursuit to acknowledge Him, to seek Him, and to hear from Him.

If you are going to flow in your assignment, then this is a non-negotiable. There is no compromise. The Spirit of God must be active within you, speaking to you and moving you forward in the pursuit of greatness. You should desire what God desires, which is to see His people aligned and living out their assignment.

When change happens on the inside, everything becomes aligned: your thinking, your speaking, your emotions, and your relationships. Your parenting is impacted. Your marriage is transformed. And your relationships are chosen carefully. Please understand that whatever you sow in your heart will be manifested in all areas of your life, including your relationships.

On the Scale Again

This journey has connected me with the lives of women who have battled with their weight. I met a woman who became ill. As a consequence, the medication she was taking contributed to her weight gain. She found herself in a place she had never been before. Not only was she battling with a health issue that had taken a toll on her body, but her state of mind was being affected as well. She had become depressed and suicidal. She told me that every day she looked at herself in the mirror and felt disgusted and ashamed. Feeling as though God had abandoned her, she contemplated taking her life. She was in a spiritual battle. Everything was magnified, as her heart was displaced. She became so consumed with her ailment and physical appearance that she lost sight of her true identity. She lost sight of her worth. Mental chaos will always manifest itself in physical form.

A friend invited this woman to the Fit for My Assignment Facebook group page. She began reading the posts of women who were being transformed by allowing God into their broken and at times shattered hearts. She made a decision: she too would rise up and ask God to change her.

She began by restoring her relationship with God. For the first time in three years she started to exercise. She implemented different eating choices. She started praying and reading the Word of God. After being encouraged to journal, she started doing so every night. Her thoughts and emotions on paper began to show her the reality of where she had been, but more importantly, where she was going. Today she stands strong in her faith. Her outlook has shifted. It is vibrant. It is promising. She is walking in her assignment.

You see, we may not be able to change our circumstances, but we can certainly change how those circumstances will affect us.

Beware of the Traps

The enemy sets up traps for us every day. They are set up with the intention of making us fall and deviate us from our assignment. The enemy wants our soul. He wants to rule our emotions, thoughts, and desires. He schemes a plan of attack and will go to great lengths to execute it. He waits for opportune moments when our defenses are down, so like the serpent he can strategically wrap himself around us and release his poison—a poison shot right at the heart. Like a skilled strategist, the enemy will feed off your most vulnerable moments. Some of these include:

- Guilt
- Loss of joy
- Trials
- Illness
- Resentment

- Anxiety
- Fear
- Betrayal
- Pain

When we feed these moments with a negative attitude instead of submitting them to God, they become a poison to our heart and soul. Perhaps you may feel like you have little or no control in moments like these, moments when "life" happens.

There is no question that at one moment or another each of us has endured hardship. However, not everyone becomes bitter, not everyone bleeds forever, and not everyone lives with eternal anxiety. We must rise up to the occasion and know that we are more than conquerors. We confront them, submit them to God, and allow God to take over. When we are feeling weak, we need to remind ourselves that our strength comes from the all-powerful God who dwells in us. We must live with an ongoing awareness that the simplest of issues can escalate until it grows to insurmountable proportions; that a little thought can become a big thought, and a little anger issue can become a big anger issue.

As I said before, I too used to live my life focusing on what I thought were the bigger, more obvious issues while bypassing the not-so-obvious things. These things, to me, did not seem as important. I would become angry about trivial, insignificant things. I allowed them to change my entire attitude and mood for the day, and sometimes several days. I desired to isolate myself from everyone and everything. Yet the revelation of the Spirit caused my soul to surrender to the wisdom, knowledge, and understanding of God. I realized the spirit and soul must be aligned and working in unison within me.

The intent of the soul is manifested in the physical realm, but it is the spirit man who must rule the soul. Self, therefore, has no alternative but to take on the form of godliness. When we die to self, God can now live through us, and everything changes.

I Want to Be More Like You, Lord

I have made up my mind that I want to live for God. I am in the best season of my life, not because I have arrived, but because I am in the process. I am living out my assignment. I am certainly not where I used to be. Change is occurring every day as I become more and more aware of the true goal before me: to become wholly fit for the assignment over my life. The more I know God, the more I want to be who God wants me to be. This attitude promotes godliness.

Imagine waking up to the presence of the Holy Spirit: "Good morning, Holy Spirit." Imagine recognizing Him as an active agent living inside your temple, ruling and dominating every thought, and holding captive anything that attempts to interrupt God's plan for your day. Imagine a day where the Holy Spirit is active in all areas of your life, from the moment you wake up until the moment you go to sleep.

I live this every day. My desire is for *you* to live it every day as well. I want to remind you that God wants all of you, from the inside out. He wants you to give Him your pain, struggles, secrets, faulty thinking, negative patterns, secrets, loneliness, fears, trials, anger, bitterness, and all those things you may struggle with but dare not share with anyone.

Perhaps you have not found anyone you feel you can trust with those secret areas of your life. You are crying inside. Let me assure you that God hears those cries for help. Surrender your spirit, soul, and body to Him. Let go! Let go! Let go, and let God! Do not spend one more moment captive to the thoughts, emotions, and desires that have separated you from God or delayed you from your assignment.

Unspeakable Joy

I came to the realization that God wanted me to be joyful. I am aware that this may sound a bit elementary, but this was part of God dealing with my heart issues. I had not realized in those moments when I lacked peace and in those moments when I struggled with my struggles, the Spirit of God was trying to help me understand that my heart condition was not producing joy.

Joy does not come from anything we can produce on the outside. True joy comes from knowing God. Have you ever heard people say, "If I could just have a bigger house, a better car, a better job, a better body, then I would be happy"? Well, I am sure it would make you happy, but trust me, it would only be temporary. The real questions are, Are you joyful? Or are you stressed?

What happens if the house is gone? Or you lose your job? Or you become sick? What happens to happiness? Does it go away, or does it stay planted firmly in place? True happiness is a heart that is joyful. This can only stem from a true relationship with God.

The people in Nehemiah's time were accustomed to falling prostrate and weeping at the reading of the Law. But after the rebuilding of ruined city walls, the people were gathered once again to hear the reading of the Law of Moses. Just as the people were ready to fall prostrate and weep at the hearing of what was being read, Nehemiah made a declaration: "Go and enjoy choice food and sweet drinks, and send some to those who have nothing prepared. This day is holy to our Lord. Do not grieve, for the joy of the LORD is your strength" (Neh. 8:10, NIV).

It's no wonder that if your joy is entangled to what you have—cars, houses, money, job security, relationships—the enemy will do everything possible to touch those things. He knows all too well that if he does, you will be more miserable than a teenager without social media (trust me, I have a teenager). The truth is, his objective is not to touch any of those temporal or material things. His ultimate objective is to rob you of your joy and ultimately deplete you of your strength. But if your true happiness—your joy—is solely based on who you are in Christ, despite your circumstances and what you have or do not have, he will not be able to knock you off of your assignment. Why? Because the joy of the Lord is your strength.

When God is ready to change something in our lives, the change must occur on the inside first. God's purpose for aligning us with Himself is to provide us with the tools and resources necessary to overcome any circumstance. Moreover, true happiness, meaning, and purpose will come from within rather than from any temporary material or physical means attained. It's time to renew, refocus, and reenergize. The joy of the Lord is *your* strength.

Don't Miss the Voice

I am a dreamer, and when I dream, I dream big. Actually, I dream as big as the God that I serve. Do you have dreams—dreams that you dare not share with anyone because you are afraid people would laugh? I have had those dreams. Yet sadly enough, when I neglected to care for the inner man, those dreams became impossible to fathom. My disconnect caused me to lose faith and trust. I needed to believe that God could make my dreams come true. So for a season I stopped dreaming. But God shook me up and brought me back to His Word. I was reminded, "Trust in the LORD and do good; dwell in the land and enjoy safe pasture. Delight yourself in the LORD and he will give you the desires of your heart" (Ps. 37:3–4). I realized that what I was dreaming was part of the plans God had for me. I know this because I am now living my dream. I learned that God's timing is perfect, yet we have the power to delay the plans when we are not aligned with them.

I remember one evening, years ago, a few friends gathered for a time of prayer. I was in my early twenties. I had a passion for God. I was on fire. I knew God had great plans for my life. I remember getting up from my seat and feeling the presence of God. I had tears in my eyes as I walked around the room in worship. One of my friends came to me and looked directly into my eyes. Though it caught me off guard, "This is it," I thought. "God is about to reveal through this individual my calling." My heart was racing. I was fully present in the moment. The individual proceeded to speak these words to me: "The Lord calls you Deborah, as you will be a prophetic voice. However, the Lord also wants you to know that you must learn to submit, take constructive criticism, and possess a humble spirit."

What? Are you kidding me? Here I am in the presence of God. I'm in the zone, and this is what God wants to tell me? "I do not receive this!" I told myself. This was nonsense. Ah, yes, as you can tell, God was dealing with me. He had been dealing with me; however, it took years before I fully surrendered.

Do you know why I did not receive that particular word? Because I was not convicted. You heard me correctly. I did not have conviction. I was not guilty of such a thing. I was humble, and I certainly did not have a problem taking criticism, as long as *I* believed it to be true. How dare that person have the audacity to come to me in the middle of my time with the Lord? In retrospect, the real question is, How could I have missed it?

It is clear to me now what God wanted to do then. He clearly told me, "You have an assignment." Those were the first words that came out of the mouth of the vessel God used to speak to me that day. It was the Holy Spirit at work. Isn't this what the Holy Spirit does best when He takes residence inside of us? He convicts us. Yet *I* was not willing to surrender. My flesh was the dominant force at the time, not the spirit man. Thankfully, years later, God moved in my life to such an extent that He not only brought conviction to particular areas in my life, but I also had the wisdom to heed His voice.

A Post From the Fit for Your Assignment Facebook Group

The enemy wants to cripple the army of the Lord. He will come from any angle he can, beginning with our minds. If he can make us afraid of criticism, our witness will become powerless. If he can cause us to become disgusted with ourselves, we will automatically assume everyone sees us with the same disgust. If the enemy can cause us to run to isolation, who can our lives affect?

═*Reflections*═

Your physical manifestations are but a reflection of your internal condition.

1. Can you think of some things you do that are reflective of the condition of your heart?

_____

_____

_____

_____

_____

_____

2. Are there things you struggle with? What are they? What would you like God to do about it? Write about it.

_____

_____

_____

_____

_____

_____

Chapter 6

WHATEVER YOU DON'T CONTROL, CONTROLS YOU

A man without self-control is like a city broken into
and left without walls.

« PROVERBS 25:28, RSV »

But I discipline my body and keep it under control, lest
after preaching to others I myself should be disqualified.

« 1 CORINTHIANS 9:27, ESV »

HAVE YOU EVER heard someone say, "I'm sorry. I just can't help it"? I believe this is equivalent to, "I am sorry. I do not have control over it." Let me be the first to shout out, "Guilty as charged!" I have always felt well balanced and in control of my life, yet the evidence proved otherwise. It is now clear thinking back to the onset of my journey that God was working to reveal this to me.

I remember arriving home from a conference feeling exhausted and out of breath. Every inch of my body was hurting and aching. I thought to myself, "Is this normal? It must be. I am not getting any younger. I need to slow down."

The Holy Spirit interrupted and made room for me to acknowledge the real reason for my pitiful physical condition. I had indulged in so much junk food for the past year that my body was simply manifesting the result of my poor choices.

I could hear my conscience saying, "Well, Reina, here it is. Apparently what you cannot control is controlling you."

I certainly did not want to own up to that statement. Whether I was willing to admit to it or not, it was true. It also became apparent in other areas of my life, like my temperament, thoughts, self-discipline, spiritual discipline, sleeping habits, my lack of movement, and so on. Would you trust someone lacking self-control with an important task or assignment?

There are many things in life that have the capacity to control us. Our senses, by our very nature, are constantly pulling our flesh toward earthly desires. There is a constant battle between the spirit and the flesh.

The Lord showed me that I could not preach beyond those areas where I lacked control. In other words, I was limiting my assignment. I could only go so far until I brought back into alignment my lack of self-control.

I knew I had to do something quickly. The more I thought about it, the more I wanted the change. I knew that the Spirit of God was eager to get started in readjusting my lack of control in very specific areas. I was ready to care for myself.

Truly, nothing can really change in your life unless you yourself make up your mind. A determined spirit is a restless spirit until it has acquired the goal it has set forth.

I was going to start over. I *wanted* to start over. God was completely on my side, and I was ready for all that God wanted to do in my life. It is a great feeling when you know you are getting your life in order. The Bible says, "I will instruct you and teach you in the way you should go; I will counsel you with my eye upon you" (Ps. 32:8, ESV).

Let me tell you what I have learned about self-control. To have self-control is to possess the ability to resist and set boundaries. It is knowing when to say no. Whom are we kidding? We live in a world of temptations—a world that is dressed to entice our senses. Our minds are inundated with images of every kind.

I was speaking to someone not too long ago about the current state of our nation. I remember a time when we had limited television channels to choose from, and by a certain hour there was nothing available to watch. Every channel went off the air, and television programs would resume in the morning. Remember those days? This is certainly not the case anymore. We now live in an era of unlimited choices. There is a channel for everything under the sun. It is difficult to learn the concept of setting limits in a world without limits.

We do not have to search far to figure out if there are areas controlling us. All it requires is for us to undertake self-examination, both internally and externally. The enemy wants nothing more than for us to succumb to the limitless supply of indulgences and temptations. The more out of control we are, the more control we have given to the enemy. This is why it is important to take the time to truly evaluate ourselves by taking a good introspective look and being honest with ourselves. As a matter of fact, we need to begin to live in such a way that no bad behavior, expression, or action goes unnoticed.

I would personally say that the journey to self-control is not easy. It is not easy to walk away from temptations. I don't know what things tempt you. But for me, I had no discipline when it came to certain types of foods, even though I knew they were not good for me. Those delectable things like pizza, french fries, bread, and my absolute weakness, chips, tempted me like unattended jewelry tempts a thief. There was nothing worse than going out to eat with friends who knew how to make the right choices. There I sat, ordering from the grease bar, while they ordered meals from the fifty-calorie section of the menu.

I have a friend who changed all her eating habits. She shared with me how God had been dealing with her in this area. She said every day for her is about controlling what her flesh wants and her spirit needs. I love that. It clicked. It made perfect sense.

We either feed our wants or feed our needs. Needs are things that are required for our survival. Wants are simply desires or added bonuses for your fleshly pleasures. I am not saying there is anything wrong with wanting things, but when we live our lives seeking to satisfy our wants and not our needs, we get into big, big trouble.

Run

There are people who do not easily fall into the traps of temptation. These are individuals who know how to set boundaries. These are the people who know that they have come too far to allow one moment of pleasure to empty them of all that God has poured in. Do you know anyone like this? Perhaps it is you. Maybe a friend? When I think of self-control, I often think of Joseph of the Hebrew Scriptures.

The Bible says, "Now Joseph was well-built and handsome, and after a while his master's wife took notice of Joseph and said, 'Come to bed with me!'" (Gen. 39:6–7). Joseph refused the temptation. As matter of fact, he responded, "'With me in charge...my master does not concern himself with anything in the house; everything he owns he has entrusted to my care. No one is greater in this house than I am. My master has withheld nothing from me except you, because you are his wife. How then could I do such a wicked thing and sin against God?' And though she spoke to Joseph day after day, he refused to go to bed with her or even be with her" (vv. 8–10).

It is clear Joseph possessed an understanding that he was a man on assignment. There are some critical points worth noting. Joseph was successful in his assignment. The Lord was with him. Everything that was placed in Joseph's hands prospered. He was successful. Joseph was a man who had favor. Imagine that—on assignment, successful, and endowed with favor. Wait, let's not forget, Joseph was one good-looking man!

Now, what did Joseph do to obtain favor and have success?

He was fit for his assignment. He was spiritually aligned. This is the same young man who was betrayed by his brothers. He was stripped of the coat his father had made especially for him. But his brothers could not strip Joseph of the God that was within him. Joseph simply knew how to say no to anything that would cause him to deviate from his God-given assignment. Was this because he had his eye on a prize? Was he striving for a position? No. His heart was simply aligned with the God he served, and everything else followed.

When your heart is right, people can do you wrong, but you will remain upright. You will remain faithful through the circumstances. You acknowledge that greater is the God in you than the force outside of you. Be reminded that the One who reigns over your spirit controls your heart. Therefore in times of temptation, self has to submit itself to the ruling of the Spirit of God that resides in you.

Joseph knew he had been entrusted with much. More importantly, his favor was in direct proportion to his stewardship and obedience. Joseph recognized boundaries. He understood limitations. He knew that there were areas he was not permitted to entertain. His master had given him specific orders regarding what things he had access to, and Joseph obeyed. Unlike Eve, who could not exert self-control when the serpent enticed her to eat from the tree of life, Joseph obeyed.

I wonder how many men would do what Joseph had done. Potiphar's wife wanted to sleep with Joseph. While Joseph was on assignment, Potiphar's wife caught Joseph by his cloak and without hesitation demanded he sleep with her. This was a woman who knew what *she* wanted—and she wanted Joseph. How did Joseph respond? This is the best part. He ran for his life!

Now some may ask, "Well, if he was disciplined and had self-control, could he not have responded, 'Woman, I will not sleep with you'?" No! Why? Let me remind you that the characters in Scripture were as human as you and I. Joseph was a man! I would venture to guess that he was a man with all his senses and masculinity working in their proper order. Furthermore, Potiphar's wife was a beautiful woman. Joseph gave Potiphar's wife the reason he would not sleep with her. Her husband had withheld her from Joseph, and Joseph did not want to sin against God. Sounds perfectly clear to me.

Joseph was determined. He refused to entertain the invitation. He said no to adultery. Perhaps he ran because he knew that if he stayed, the flesh would win. He had made up his mind that he was not going to sin. Better yet, he wasn't going to have a conversation with sin. This is important; he had made up his mind. He denied self in obedience to the God he knew. The taste of obedience became more enticing than the taste of sin.

Self-control is being able to deny self when self is pushing in the direction it should not go. One must possess great strength. This strength can only come from God. Your willingness is as powerful as the God who lives in you. It is when we get to this place of deep discipline that we know the inner spirit man is aligned with God. When you are confronted by sin and don't know what to do, RUN!

I've Got the Power

> For God did not give us a spirit of fear, but of power and of love and of self-control.
>
> —2 TIMOTHY 1:7, BBE

We have the power to control our tempers, our emotions, the way we speak, the way we think, the way we act, and, yes, even the decisions we make. When we lack control in these areas, it means we lack a sound mind and the ability to reason effectively. When issues affect the mind, it is difficult to make sound, godly decisions. When we cannot stop to reason, we act impulsively. When we act impulsively, we are in essence allowing self to take control. When we do, we move forward without thinking of the ramifications.

God does not want us to move in our assignments with impulsive and out-of-control behaviors. God does not want us to be controlled by anything other than the power of the Holy Spirit that lives in us. We need to use the power God has given us. Our sanity depends on it. The place God has prepared for us requires us to think, speak, and act rationally.

Have you ever been really angry? I confess that there have been times people have given me some very good reasons to be angry. At least, this is how I justified my anger. There have been occasions where I have invested time and energy in people who have turned around and done the very opposite of what I counseled them to do, only to find themselves back in my office seeking additional help. Other times I have felt what I refer to as "spiritual anger," a zeal for God so intense that when I see people go back into the same pit God pulled them out of, I feel angry.

But have you gotten so angry that you have lost all sense of reasoning? I have seen people lose jobs, homes, and relationships because they were unable to control their anger. A lack of self-control can destroy us, our assignments, families, and relationships with God.

Are these important to you? Is there an area where you know that if you do not act quickly, you can potentially cause great harm to yourself and those you love? Let me encourage you. God has given you the power to step out of the confines of fear and walk into the realm of self-control.

The enemy likes to scare us by telling us we have no power over our circumstances. He tells us we cannot change who we are any more than we can change the things that have happened. Do not believe it! The enemy is the great deceiver and the father of lies. Turn your heart toward God and away from the circumstances. The moment you turn your heart toward God, you will change who you are, because you will change how you see yourself.

Charles Spurgeon wrote, "It is well for us that, amidst all the variableness of life, there is One whom change cannot affect; One whose heart can never alter, and one whose brow mutability can make no furrows."[1]

Controlling Anger

One of the most rewarding assignments in my life, alongside being a mom, is being a wife. If you are married, then you have an assignment and responsibility toward your spouse. You are called to minister to each other's spirit and deal with issues together. Too often I've witnessed relationships become really ugly when one person is aligned with God and the other is not.

There have been occasions when I have become angry at my spouse because I did not get my way. Yes, I suffered from this too. I did tell you that your heart condition would spill into all areas of your life. Now, I have the best husband a girl could ask for. As a matter of fact, his patience demands an award for all the temper tantrums he has had to put up with, especially in the early years of our marriage. If he were reading this right now, he would probably shout, "Amen!"

We both were aware early on in our relationship that God had a great assignment over our lives. From the onset we decided that God would reign in our home and in our hearts. There was little we could get away with because conviction was prevalent. If there was chaos, you better believe conviction followed. In disagreements and in times of trials the presence of God would not let our spirits rest until we made things right. I am so thankful for that.

God is simply amazing. When you make God the King of your heart, you can rest assured that He has your best interest in mind. He watches over your soul, cares for it, and nurtures it; moreover, He stirs it until there is acknowledgment of wrongdoing, followed by reconciliation.

A display of anger is only a camouflage for the pain inside a wounded soul. This is not healthy anger by any means. This is poison to the soul if not controlled. The magnitude of anger displayed is often in direct proportion to the magnitude of hidden things inside your soul.

Anger has left many wounded soldiers in the battlefield. One day you will go back to the battlefield and realize that your misdirected, unhealthy anger has crushed spirits, including yours.

I have seen angry parents speak in anger to their children, spewing words that have pierced their fragile souls. I have seen couples share hard, piercing words with each other that have been carried into their marriages for years.

Maybe you were told that you were not good enough, that you were ugly and unworthy of love. Maybe you have been abused and mistreated. For years you have been covering the wounds that are so ever present in your heart. Every time someone mistakenly touches your wounds, you bleed. The pain is so excruciating, you just cannot control your reaction.

How long will you live having to rebandage a wound that refuses to heal unless there is divine intervention? Take off that bandage for good. Let God rest His hands on the wound, and watch Him make the bleeding stop. Yes, it may hurt, and you will feel the pressure, but when all is said and done, that wound will no longer affect you. The scars may stay, but they will become reminders of what you have overcome. You are going to make it through. I know it. I have seen people come out of the rubble of despair victoriously.

The best way to rid oneself of unhealthy displays of anger is to do the following:

- Expose the anger and take the bandage off.
- Tell God to take you to the root.
- Don't do it alone. Find someone who will pray you through it.
- Seek counsel. There are layers to peel, and you need someone with experience to guide you through the process.
- Be free of guilt.
- Trust God; trust the process.

Oh, what a loving God we have. There is nothing so horrible that we can do to turn Him away. When we sin, the Holy Spirit convicts us—not to condemn us, but to restore and remind us of the greatness inside of us. It works like this:

Imagine hearing consistently, "You were made for greatness," or, "The plans I have for you are to prosper you." Imagine from the moment you wake up until you close your eyes at night, these words are impressed in your spirit. Now imagine the sin you hold in your life colliding with the Holy Spirit's declaration for you. You are convicted. The conviction is so strong that there is no more room for the sin because you possess an awareness of the greatness of God in you. Now sin has to go in order to make room for the greatness and plans God has for you. This is how a sovereign and loving God works.

Controlling What Comes Out of Our Mouths

Women are emotional beings by nature. This has been a really good excuse used to get away with bad behavior. I can almost hear the average man reading this right now shouting, "Hallelujah! Isn't that the truth?" Emotions are fleeting and unstable, and you cannot depend on them. As a matter of fact, crimes of passion have often been a consequence of emotions gone haywire. Displaced emotions have caused affairs, broken marriages, ministry failures, loss of jobs, and illnesses. The things that come out of our mouths in times of anger leave us perplexed when our anger dissipates, our reasoning returns, and we are able to reflect. Being fit for your assignment means controlling what comes out of your mouth.

Have you ever said something, only to regret it the second after you said it? I have done this one too many times. I am not perfect, so I have to confess that once in a while I still say some things I wished I had not said. This is why, to keep my tongue under submission, each morning I go before God and say, "Lord, keep me from offending or hurting anyone. May I think before I speak."

The Book of Proverbs says, "Whoever keeps his mouth and his tongue keeps himself out of trouble" (Prov. 21:23, ESV).

Whatever it is that you cannot control ultimately controls you. It is time to put God back into the driver's seat and allow Him to take hold of your thoughts, emotions, and desires. You will not be able to serve the needs of others effectively as long as you lack self-control. Make God your motivation, and do not give up. Get started right away. God is going to give you the courage, because He has given you the power.

Here's to living a life of self-control:

- Turn your heart toward God.

- Call on the Holy Spirit.

- Do not justify bad behavior; get to the root of it.

- Pray.

- Make God your motivation.

- Put on courage.

- Do not give up.

A Post From the Fit for Your Assignment Facebook Group

 I am proud of myself today. I was able to keep my thoughts on self-control and therefore was able to accomplish what I needed to do. I am activating the Word.

⇒ *Reflections* ⇐

The more out of control you are, the more in control the enemy is.

1. Do you feel self-control is important for your assignment? Why?

_____

_____

_____

_____

_____

2. When you hear the word *self-control*, what comes to mind?

_____

_____

_____

_____

_____

SECTION TWO
THE FOUR PRINCIPLES OF GETTING FIT FOR YOUR ASSIGNMENT

GOD GAVE ME four principles that would forever change my life. These principles moved me into complete alignment. I believe they will do the same for you. The four principles are conviction, confrontation, revelation, and transformation. Are you ready? This is where the plot really thickens. Thus far I've been laying a foundation, but this is where the rubber meets the road.

When you understand these principles, you will find yourself applying them to all areas of your life. The moment I was confronted by the Holy Spirit, I was convicted of the need for inner healing. God took me by the hand and walked me to every area that needed change. The rug was pulled from under me, and I had to confront each issue separately. I was being given the revelation to deal with each issue, and time was of the essence. The moment I dealt with my issues, a transformation occurred within that allowed me to see with clarity what I had never seen before. God was revealing His true purpose for my life. There were things I did not yet know or understand about myself, and there were certainly things I did not know about the God whom I served. But when I entered the realm of the unknown, I knew I would never be the same again.

Are you ready to receive the Spirit's direction for your life? Wait until you discover the greater plan. *Your* life will never be the same again.

Turn the page. It is time to discover some more.

Chapter 7

STEP 1: CONVICTION

And when he comes, he will convict the world concerning sin and righteousness and judgment.

« JOHN 16:8, ESV »

Conviction [Greek: *elegcho*]: to reprove, to expose, to convince, show fault, or to call into account.[1]

GOD SHOWED UP when I least expected it. I felt His presence as it moved me from my comfort zone and placed me in the midst of my own barrenness. His hand was heavy upon my soul. It was difficult to understand the profoundness of what was happening. His words pierced my heart, as grief overcame me—a grief that stemmed from the loss I had never mourned until that moment. When had it died—my passion, my zeal, my discipline, and my love for self? For the first time I was convicted of the real issues that were keeping me stagnant. What I had just experienced was conviction. I was awakened to an awareness that brought me to a place of total exposure.

To better understand conviction, let's journey to Isaiah chapter 6. The prophet Isaiah is about to receive his assignment from the Lord, but not before he is convicted in his heart. Let's look at this closely:

> I saw the Lord sitting upon a throne, high and lifted up; and the train of his robe filled the temple.
>
> —ISAIAH 6:1, ESV

Perhaps Isaiah had been grieving his king. The king died a tragic death, and now what? What an opportunity for God to demonstrate His glory—His very nature. Isaiah finds himself without a king. The throne is empty. Yet the King of kings is still sitting on the throne. Isaiah may have been disheartened by the loss of a king, but what he now sees pierces right to the heart. He is gripped in worship he had never heard before. A presence had filled the house. The Lord, presence, and worship—something is about to happen to Isaiah.

Wherever there is true worship, the presence of God abides. Wherever God makes His presence known, hearts are stirred. We cannot hide from the presence of God. It is in the presence of God that our hearts reflect our true state of being. Isaiah's conviction was great, as he said:

> Woe is me, for I am undone; because I am a man of unclean lips, and I dwell in the midst of a people of unclean lips: for my eyes have seen the King, Jehovah of hosts.
>
> —ISAIAH 6:5, ASV

Ah, yes, conviction at its best. Isaiah proclaims that he is undone; that was the good news. Now God is able to do something even greater in his life. He recognizes he needs God. He recognizes his sin. His eyes are opened to his sin as well as the sin of the people. His eyes are opened to the need that others have for the God he sought after and increasingly needed. Isaiah was not a bad man. He was a prophet. But he needed a face-to-face encounter with a righteous and holy God.

When we come into alignment with God, we are exposed to His sovereignty. Before Isaiah could walk in his assignment, God brought him to a place of confession: "I am man of unclean lips."

Isaiah recognized that he may have said and done things that were not pleasing to God.

Wait, was he not a prophet? One of the good guys? I have news for you: even the good guys need to experience God's conviction. Conviction gives us an understanding, a knowing that no matter what we do while we are in these earthly vessels, at any given moment we could fail God. We may fail Him in our words, conduct, or our assignment. Isaiah recognized where he had failed. God cleansed him and gave him orders for his next assignment.

While the voice of conviction hovered over me, the Lord began to bring to the surface various scenarios in my life, scenarios that for a long time remained hidden under the covers of my busy ministerial life. It wasn't until I was exposed to conviction that I realized that preaching and teaching four or five times per week in addition to my speaking engagements outside of my local church was becoming more of a routine and less of a passion. As a matter of fact, I was tending to everything in body, but my spirit was far from engaged. This is not how God intended my life to be lived, yet this was my harsh reality.

We cannot escape conviction. Conviction comes when God makes His entrance into our heart. Conviction does two things: it provides an awareness of the availability of God's grace and mercy over our lives, and it brings us into war within ourselves. In the midst of being convicted, we become quite uncomfortable if there are areas that are not aligned. As holiness is revealed, we become alarmed by the sinfulness that resides within.

Addressing conviction, Oswald Chambers writes:

> Conviction of sin is one of the rarest things that ever strikes a man. It is the threshold of an understanding of God. Jesus Christ said that when the Holy Spirit came He would convict of sin, and when the Holy Spirit rouses a man's conscience and brings him back into the presence of God, it is not his relationship with men that bothers him, but his relationship with God.[2]

Did you capture the profoundness of this revelation? The presence of God will cause us to search the relationship we have with Him. The Holy Spirit brings us into His very presence, and in absolute surrender we yield our hearts to God.

Conviction is not merely to expose our detrimental state of being. Rather, it is designed to help us understand that God wants to restore us back to Him. As a result, we walk in obedience and live to please God as we serve others. Hence, the movement of our everyday living helps to provoke transformation in others.

As the Holy Spirit comes to bring about communion with God, it will cause us to reevaluate all that we have done up until that moment.

Recalling the infamous April afternoon when I stood before the mirror, I have one word to describe how I felt. *Disrobed.* I felt as if someone had completely exposed me to myself and I had nowhere to hide. I thought I could walk away and go on living life as usual. Whom was I kidding? The Holy Spirit had His hand of conviction upon me and would not let me go.

After what I believed was an amazing evening at the conference, I sat in my office, took my shoes off, and stared at my computer. I could feel the Holy Spirit pressing on my heart. I wanted to run. I wanted to hide. I wanted so badly to shake it off. As horrible as it felt at the time, it is the best thing that happened to me. I felt as if God had made a list of everything that needed to change and laid it out before me.

I could feel and hear the Spirit of God tugging at the core of my soul asking me, "Where have you been? Where is your passion? Where is your zeal for excellence? When did it change?"

"Oh, Lord, please stop," I cried out.

What was He doing? He was going to give me what I had asked for. I had asked Him to reveal His great plan for my life. I had asked Him to mold me, to change me. I told Him I was going to move forward in all He had for me. I said I would move without fear. Yes, but that was months ago. I had forgotten. Truly, how could I underestimate the power of a praying woman? I had invited His presence. I had invited His Spirit to take my heart and do as He saw fit. He did, and He showed me that I had allowed life to take a toll on my spirit. I had neglected to take care of it.

Although we love God, family, and all that we do, a moment arrives in our lives where we want to wake up to something different. This moment may be enthused by feeling a lack of appreciation, defeated, or lonely, to name a few. Interestingly enough, it may occur while you are surrounded by people who support and love you. I was there. The enemy had made the little issues in my life quite grand, and they had developed into full-grown monsters.

The enemy's agenda was to paralyze me. He wanted to stop the assignment over my life and hold my thoughts captive in fear and defeat. I refused to talk about it with anyone. If I talked about it, then I was affirming it. I wanted to believe these were small issues that would not affect me. I didn't realize that not talking about them had contributed to the destructive plan of attack. These issues did not come all at once. They showed up as random preoccupations, moments of fear, an occasional meltdown, and so forth.

Note that the enemy was subtle in his approach. It wasn't apparent until some of these feelings became part of my everyday thought process. It was evident that something was wrong. The one thing I refused to continue with was the lack of passion for what I loved to do—deliver God's Word to His people. I knew I had to do something.

So for a year I did not accept any speaking engagements outside of my church. From a public perception I did not have a legitimate excuse for taking a year off. However, God knew the reason. I needed *my* God to deal with me. I needed to confront some issues that perhaps to some were insignificant, but I knew that in order to do what God had required of me, I had to confront them.

I took a semester off from graduate school. I cleared my schedule. I had an appointment with God, and I did not know how long it was going to take. But I was ready.

Conviction had arrived, and there was no greater feeling than being reunited with God's presence. That inner conviction stirred the Spirit of God, and His presence manifested itself through all my sense of reasoning. I came before God and cried in repentance. His presence drew me close to Him, revealing His everlasting and unconditional love. Only God can penetrate our hearts like a double-edged sword and a healing balm all at once. He took me by the hand and led me beside still waters. I was thirsty for righteousness, and the Shepherd of shepherds knew exactly where I needed to be.

I had wasted too much time entertaining the enemy and his schemes. My spirit had been in slumber. God wanted to accelerate me, yet issues that I ignored kept me from moving forward. But the time had come, and the time was now. Conviction had arrived, and it waited for me to throw open the doors of my heart and align myself to the assignment before me.

I want to impress in your spirit that it is imperative to take an inventory of your life. Do not neglect your spirit man. Do not turn your head away from the small issues. I can assure you they are deadly. They slowly eat away at your spirit. Take a really close look at your life. Yes, take a moment. Are there any areas that you feel lack balance? Does something seem strangely off course? Stop! Take a closer look. What have those things stopped you from accomplishing? What are the thoughts that come to mind?

In my case I was losing my passion for what I loved to do. What had I done or not done for this to happen? I needed to find the contributing factors so that I could confront and deal with them.

We have to examine ourselves and make sure we are in alignment. Don't ignore the signs. Don't be satisfied with just getting by and getting through. God has called you to live. God has called you to enjoy His presence and be passionate about what you do. It is passion that will keep you focused in the midst of the most difficult testing times.

I am not saying that being aligned with God means that all pain and issues are gone. I am saying that being aligned with God will help you be prepared to handle any situation that comes your way. Being aligned with God helps you to realize that *He* is your strong tower. In addition, the Holy Spirit will be dwelling in a temple that is in order and ready to fulfill a God-given assignment.

Have you ever felt stuck? You know, stuck in the same place while others are moving forward? Stuck while others are growing in God, in blessings, provision, open doors, and favor? I too have felt like this. I know few people who deny they have wondered why God delays some things. It wasn't until I completely surrendered to God that, almost immediately, I began to experience open doors I would have never thought would open otherwise. I began to see the fulfillment of dreams that only God knew about.

What made the difference? Prior to my year of complete conviction, confrontation, revelation, and transformation I was serving God on my terms. This is what I mean by *my* way of serving. God was still doing good things in my life, because this is just who God is. He will not stop blessing us. I really do not believe He has the character to stop. Why would He? That would make Him like us. God's love is unconditional toward us. We will never understand His ways, as His ways are higher than our ways.

I was not wholly fit, and so I was not a good steward of what God had deposited inside of me. As God raised awareness via the Holy Spirit, I transcended to a place of revelation where I understood the importance of the greater plan for my life.

As a result, I am freed from religious beliefs, most of which I myself conjured up in an attempt to believe I was pleasing God. You know the kind of beliefs I'm talking about: "I am supposed to do this," or, "I am not supposed to do that."

God filled me with His love and righteousness so that I could pursue all that is right. I became transparent and allowed others to see God working in and through me. My posture changed as I now have a newfound relationship with God. I knew *about* Him then, but now I feel like I know Him—really know Him. I felt like Job (although I didn't endure all he endured) when he declared, "I had heard of you by the hearing of the ear, but now my eye sees you" (Job 42:5, ESV). I had an encounter with God.

Don't let the word *conviction* scare you. Conviction is not the same as condemnation. Condemnation says there is no hope for you. It seeks to point out your sins and bring guilt. Conviction says God sees the greatness in you and wants to bring you to an intimate encounter with Him. Condemnation seeks to accuse you; conviction seeks to vindicate you. Condemnation is full of religious dogma; conviction is full of relational direction. Condemnation tears down; conviction builds up. You get the point.

I know of someone who was going through a series of circumstances. I mean it was downright pouring in her life—and they weren't showers of blessings. It felt as though there was thunder and lightning at the turn of every day. You know the adage "when it rain it pours"?

This individual was not easily knocked down. Community service and engagement was her main forte. That kind of service bought her joy and fulfillment, and no one was going to change that. This person was on assignment and focused. I noticed, however, that this individual's demeanor was changing. She was still engaged in the work and assignment, yet somehow she seemed different.

Weeks later this person confessed to being addicted to pornography, and that conviction had hit so hard that the spirit of this individual became restless. This person knew that confession needed to happen and accountability was a must if the battle with this addiction was going to be won. After she spoke about it and made plans for corrective measures, peace replaced the anxiety and restlessness of the soul.

I was most impressed by the courage this person had to move on the conviction deep within. The conviction was so compelling that sin could no longer reside. The ability to overcome and conquer was a consequence of heeding the tugging of the Holy Spirit and knowing that dependency relied on God alone.

Do you see how important it is to act on convictions? It frees us to return to God's original plan for our lives. We will battle, and some will battle more than others. We are not free of attacks. However, as the Holy Spirit moves inside and as we care and nurture the spirit man, we will be prepared to face the challenges and come forth victorious.

Love Your Neighbor as You Love Yourself

Serving others does not mean forgetting about self. I have heard many messages and studies on the passage of Scripture relating to loving our neighbors as we love ourselves. (See Mark 12:31, GW.) Most often the focus is on "loving your neighbor." While this is God's Word—and I certainly receive it—I cannot bypass the second half, which says, "as you love yourself."

What does loving myself mean? I had to ask God, because this verse had been laid heavily in my spirit. I knew God wanted to give me a revelation. As God dealt with me, this portion of Scripture became more relevant and more precise.

Suppose you find out someone you love is hurting or neglecting areas of their life. Would you ignore it? Would you never address it? Or would you do whatever is in your power to address the issues and help the person heal?

I know I would not walk past it and pretend it doesn't exist. As a matter of fact, my love for the person would obligate me to stop and pay attention to the need. The motivation? Love. Love addresses issues. Love surrenders to change. Love isn't selfish. Love acts!

This is one area in which God convicted me. He asked me, "How can you love others like you say you do, when you don't love yourself to care enough about the issues of your spirit, soul, and body?" It became clear that if I was called to love my neighbor, then I needed to love *me* first. I needed to take care of my issues right away.

Self-care became a priority. We must be good to ourselves. We are the vessels God has chosen to carry *His* assignment. When the inner man is taken care of, everything else flows in harmony.

So I made a decision. I was going to focus more on my inner appearance. What good was it to have a nice, tailored suit with the right shoes and accessories to match if the inner man was a mess?

I encourage you to pray and ask God to convict you and present you with a clear picture of your total self. There is nothing to fear and everything to be gained. I know this because I live it every day. Ask yourself important questions such as the following:

- Am I where God wants me to be?
- How is my spiritual life?
- Do I take time to care for the issues of my heart?
- Do I practice self-care?
- When was the last time I felt conviction?

I have seen so many come to God in repentance as they receive the conviction that has thrust them into the righteousness of God.

As you enter the realm of deeper understanding and revelation, the Holy Spirit will endow you with wisdom to carry your assignment to full term.

I speak to the spirit man inside you, "Arise, shine, for your light has come, and the glory of the LORD rises upon you" (Isa. 60:1).

A Post From the Fit for Your Assignment Facebook Group

His presence is more than enough! God has been preparing my heart within these last few days to praise despite the pain, because healing and restoration come when we exalt His name.

⇒ *Reflections* ⇐

God wants to restore us back to Him.

1. Self-care is important. God wants us to take care of ourselves. What are some things you can do to provide self-care? Go ahead and list them, then make a plan to implement them.

_____

_____

_____

_____

_____

_____

2. Write how this chapter on conviction has impacted you.

_____

_____

_____

_____

_____

_____

Chapter 8

STEP 2: CONFRONTATION

But the one who does not know and does things deserving punishment will be beaten with few blows. From everyone who has been given much, much will be demanded; and from the one who has been entrusted with much, much more will be asked.

《 LUKE 12:48 》

Confront: "To come face to face with."[1]

IN 2 SAMUEL 12:7 we find that King David is being confronted by the prophet Nathan because David has committed adultery. As a result, Bathsheba, the woman with whom he has committed adultery, has become pregnant. David makes an attempt to blame her pregnancy on Bathsheba's rightful husband, Uriah, who has just come back from war.

This blame shifting is really an attempt at concealing David's sin of adultery. His plan backfires as Uriah refuses to fall for the trap. David puts Uriah in a compromising military position, where he ultimately gets killed. Now that Uriah is dead, David takes Uriah's wife, Bathsheba, now conveniently a widow, to be *his* wife. Here we have a great king with a God-given assignment giving in to the desires of the flesh.

David may have thought he could move on with his life. God,

however, had other plans. God needed to confront David. David's assignment was not finished, and he had been chosen, anointed, and blessed for this assignment. God had given much to David—and to whom God has given much, much is required.

God did not want David to live with hidden secrets in the chambers of his heart. Just as He dealt with David, He deals with us. He exposes us to the unresolved issues that delay the call and purpose over our lives. The enemy wants nothing more than to keep us from moving forward in life. He attempts to instill fear, guilt, and regret. He desires to keep us confined and stagnant. We cannot be afraid, however, to deal with the situations of life. Confrontation is not a means to condemn us, nor is it to remind us of our failures! Far from it. Confrontation opens the door for us to receive restoration and spiritual alignment.

There will come a point in our lives where we must encounter a face-off with past unhealthy behaviors, habits, and faulty thinking. We must be willing to deal with it all! We cannot pick and choose what we are willing to tackle. We must ask God to give us courage to embrace all that God wants us to change. We need to examine those areas and cry out to God, "What have I done to hinder, stagnate, and slow down the assignment?" Allow the Holy Spirit to speak to your heart, and like David, confess, "Lord, I have sinned against You."

David's spirit was awakened to the reality that he had sinned against God. The prophet Nathan confronted him, and when David realized the heart-wrenching truth, he immediately opened his mouth and confessed. The flesh had provoked him to sin. Yet Nathan let him know that God had already forgiven him. Were there consequences? Absolutely. There are consequences to everything we do. It does not mean, however, that we remain in a pit of despair. We must let go and keep moving.

God stands before us, never leaving us to deal with our issues alone. He wants us to be free of those things that linger in the corners of our soul. God wants us to be free—free to worship Him, free to move in our assignment, and free to live a full and rich life where our dreams come together with God's desire to create our destiny. As our hearts become aligned to His will, we are endowed with His dreams and desires.

A few chapters back I shared with you that for me, confrontation came through like a tsunami. Everything I thought I had in order was suddenly displaced, and all I could see before me was disarray. If I was going to confront some things, then I had to trust that God was going to prepare my heart to receive the painful truths about some of these areas in my life. And that He did. I knew that I did not want to live in such chaos any longer. As a matter of fact, my spirit would not allow it. I had been stirred and awakened to a new and improved mind-set. I had experienced God differently. It was an intimate, personal experience. He had spoken directly to my heart, and I knew that there were treasures waiting for me: open doors, opportunities, new habits, a new relationship with Him, and a deeper revelation.

If you are going to be fit for all that God is getting ready to do in your life, it is time to come face-to-face with some issues. There is no room for fear. As a matter of fact, the moment you are ready to step into the ring and confront some of your issues, you will discover that God is already present.

How the Lord Led Me to Start the Fit for Your Assignment Thirty-Day Challenge

During one of my prayer times the Lord impressed in my heart to start a thirty-day challenge toward becoming fit for my assignment. This challenge would include spiritual, physical, and emotional alignment. I encouraged the ladies on our Facebook group page to join me. We started by posting "before" pictures of ourselves. I took a full-body picture and submitted it to the group. The ladies followed suit. Everyone was excited. There was much momentum. We were going to be accountable to each other. Everyone was eager to get started.

As I prepared to lead and take on this challenge, I asked God to reveal His heart to us each day. There were more than seven hundred women taking the challenge—a relatively large number considering this was a small, private group. My work was cut out for me, and I was excited. Everyone was embracing the challenge enthusiastically. As I read posts from women all over the country each day, challenging themselves to become fit in every area, I was blessed.

Every day I rose early in the morning, and before getting ready for the office, I would post a scripture and a challenge for that particular day. I encouraged each woman to embrace the day, meet the challenge, pray, and memorize the day's scripture. I also encouraged them to journal their experiences at the end of each day. I realized God was further setting me up to pick up some new habits and break some old ones. God was ready to confront me as I encouraged others to confront their issues.

As days passed, most women were up for the challenges. The first week I told each woman to create a collage that best represented her. I also told them to journal the feelings and emotions they felt when creating their collages.

Well, the ladies started posting their collages and sharing their experiences. But there was a problem—I had yet to create my collage.

The first week of the challenge had yet to culminate when I felt the Holy Spirit tugging at my heart saying, "Reina, how about you? Have you prayed? Did you memorize your scripture? And where is your collage?"

Yes, God required more of me.

Did I think I could get away with it? At that moment I didn't see anything wrong with it. I was going to do it, but I would do it during my "free" time. Here I was again, telling God I would do it on my time and on my terms. Whom was I kidding? I rarely had free time. Procrastination had risen up and shown its face. I had encouraged the ladies to complete their challenge, and I had yet to start mine. The Lord confronted me with the fact that I had become an expert procrastinator over the last few years. I had missed opportunities. But that was about to change. I was not willing to spend another year without being fit! I determined to resolve all my issues.

I realized God had set me up to initiate the thirty-day challenge so that I would confront some areas in my life. Did I think that God was going to wait for me to get it all together to start me off on a new assignment? No!

You see, God's ways are not our ways; His ways are so much higher. He gave me a new assignment and used the assignment to promote alignment in my life. At this juncture in my journey I thought I had dealt with all that needed to be dealt with.

There is no question that if we are going to straighten up from our crooked ways, we often need to come to God for spiritual alignment. We can't become so "spiritual" that we feel we don't need God to bring us into alignment every now and then. As a matter of fact, every time we bend our knees to pray or open our mouths to worship, we should invite God to bring spiritual alignment to all areas of our lives.

For thirty days I needed to stay consistent and focused. I needed to pray each morning, read Scripture, and listen to my heart as to what the daily challenge would be. As you can see, God was moving me out of stagnation and breaking the spirit of procrastination.

It was about one o'clock in the morning one day when I boldly declared, "Procrastination, this is the last time you are part of me. I am doing away with you. You will no longer have control of me!"

The moment I called it by name, not only did I deal with it, but also I identified it. I knew what was hindering me, and I knew that it could destroy my purpose. I was not willing to allow procrastination to delay me any longer.

Procrastination had to go because there were things God desired me to do—and do them now. Those things could not wait. Time was of the essence.

If we are going to change, it needs to be now. If the Spirit of God prompts us, this is a good indicator that activation must be initiated *now* and not tomorrow. We can't settle with waiting until tomorrow, or waiting until we feel we are ready.

I had a responsibility to these ladies, to myself, and to God. Did I really think I could set my own time frame to fulfill the assignments for which God held me responsible? No! I needed to seize every God-moment, and I needed to begin now.

Details Matter

It matters that we are on time with our assignment. Many of us come from different walks of life and with different assignments. I am assigned to two beautiful daughters whom God has given me to care for and nurture. Some time ago I read a book titled *The Year of Magical Thinking.*

Joan Didion depicts her personal pain as she exposes the reality of illness and death. In the book she writes, "Life changes fast. Life changes in the instant. You sit down to dinner and life as you know it ends."[2]

After reading the book, I went to see the monologue on Broadway. Joan Didion, played by Vanessa Redgrave, began to describe her daughter who was battling cancer. She even described what her daughter was wearing on a particular day. Every detail from head to toe was like a portrait being painted in the canvas of my mind.

After the Broadway show I wanted to sit down and soak up the full experience of such an intense monologue. My husband and I walked to one of our favorite spots in New York City near the theater. The moment I sat down, I felt a rush of emotions overtake me. I could barely get a word out. Looking down and feeling too ashamed to look my husband in the eyes, I said, "I can't remember what my girls are wearing today." I had barely ended my sentence when I began to cry.

My husband looked at me and listened.

I had just been confronted with the reality that I had become so busy with so many other things that I had neglected my assignment as a mom. I continued, "What if something happens to them? Can I describe what they are wearing?" My heart ached; two precious jewels, and I had missed the details.

This may seem a bit extreme to you. You may be thinking, "Reina, we can't always remember what our kids are wearing. This doesn't make us bad parents."

Allow me to share my perspective. My girls were not adults. They were not living outside of my home. They were little girls, fragile vessels. I dressed them and combed their hair every morning. How could I not remember? This was a God-moment, a confrontation that demanded I deal with the situation at hand. God showed me that when we are on assignment, we must be focused on all aspects of that assignment. Each time I dressed them I was competing with time. I wasn't fully present. I was either running late or consumed with too much on my mind. Yes, I was meeting their needs, but was I giving them the very best of me? This is what God wanted me to understand. God will use any opportunity to confront us and bring us back into alignment. This does not mean I did not love my girls; it simply meant that I became sloppy in my assignment. I can honestly tell you that pivotal moment marked my life forever.

The Difference Between Conviction and Confrontation

When we think of the word *confrontation*, we often think of the negative connotations. The enemy would want us to stay away from that word. The truth is that confrontation is the exposure of something, bringing it to the forefront, and dealing with it in a bold, determined, and steadfast way. Confrontation is not so much about you confronting someone else or someone else confronting you. The kind of confrontation I am talking about is a face-to-face encounter with yourself and with God. There are no two ways about it. It is God coming face-to-face with us and telling us, "I love you so much that I want you to boldly go and confront those things that have control over you. Confront those things that are lingering in the corners of your soul."

Confrontation comes after you have been convicted of those things that have held you captive. My husband would say that confrontation is the "action" of decision making. You see, decision making begins in the mind. You can have conviction and even make a mental decision, but until you take action, you will remain in the same place you received your conviction. He would put it this way: "Vision without the decision to take action is only an illusion." I love how it sounds in Spanish: *Visión, sin la decisión de tomar una acción, es sólo una ilusión.*

Remember the parable of the prodigal son in Luke 15:11–32? There was no question that after prematurely squandering his father's inheritance, he found himself remembering the good ol' days. As he sat desiring to eat the pods that the pigs were eating, conviction kicked in. The son came to his senses and said, "I will arise" (v. 18, ESV). He made a mental decision and had to first confront himself and then confront, or face, his father in repentance. He said, "I will say to him, 'Father, I have sinned against heaven and before you'" (v. 18, ESV).

Wait; thus far the intentions are great. The mental decision making is there. But the truth is, he was still in the same place. It isn't until we see, "And he arose and came to his father..." (v. 20, ESV), that true confrontation was engaged. Don't spend your life in an illusion, thinking, *what if*: What if I would have confronted my issues? What if I would have apologized? What if I would have repented? What if I would have forgiven? You were not created for the pigpen; you were created to enjoy the blessings and freedom that come with being a child of God.

Let me take you back to the thirty-day challenge. The ladies engaged in the challenge were breezing through the first week. They were posting their testimonies. Some posted testimonies about breaking smoking habits. Others were exercising for the first time in many years. The testimonies were certainly too many for me to list here.

The first week was all about eating and physical wellness. We were pumped! And then the second week came around. This is when the tides turned.

Up until then everyone was doing fantastic. I am not suggesting that breaking bad eating patterns, breaking smoking addictions, or forming good exercise habits are easy. By no means. Here was a platform to discuss their struggles as other women would muster up the courage to be transparent and encourage one another. However, it was time for God to take this challenge to another level. We were about to expose areas of our lives that were kept hidden—some too painful to bear.

Why do we keep things that have hurt us hidden? To protect us, that's why.

In the second week of the challenge the ladies would engage in an inner examination through the means of various challenges. These would provide the opportunity for self-reflection and an opportunity to deal with matters of the heart. My goal was for women to begin exploring the "whys" of bad habits as well as other elements they felt had affected their ability to be aligned mentally, physically, and spiritually.

Throughout the challenge I discovered that women were not comfortable talking about their struggles with eating habits. Most women were willing (and some were quite eager) to discuss their relationship with food, but not the bad habits.

One morning during the second week of the challenge I presented them with a different kind of challenge, and everything changed. I asked the women to sit quietly and journal whatever came to mind. They were not allowed to think through it. They were to write without making corrections or reading back through what they had written until they were done.

Can you say, "resistance"? Some of the ladies were bold enough to say, "Absolutely not. I am not going to do it." Others were hesitant but went along with it. I did not want to force anyone to do something they were not ready to do.

One woman, however, shared her experience. She said that in

one respect, it was the most painful thing she had ever done; yet in another, it was the most liberating. She prayed and started writing. After she was done, she read back the things she had written. They were deep issues of the heart. She realized there were issues in her heart that she knew she had to deal with if she was going to be spiritually fit. The hardest part for her was coming face-to-face with all the mistakes she felt she had made in her past. She was living with the guilt of divorce, children gone astray, and personal addictions.

Like this woman, there are many people who are bound and enslaved by their past. The enemy, the great accuser, has done a fine job at keeping some folks from walking in their destiny and purpose.

Have you ever felt ashamed of something? Well, can I tell you that shame is what keeps many people from confronting their issues? The pain of wrong behaviors and foolish decisions has kept many captive in a net of denial. The internal voices sound something like this: "If I keep it hidden and tucked away. I will eventually forget about it. If I confront it, it means I am responsible, and I cannot bear to face this truth."

Some people will not come face-to-face with their issues because if they do, it only means they are obligated to validate that these things indeed happened. For some, this is very painful. They will therefore find other things to focus their efforts on rather than confront their truth.

C. S. Lewis wrote:

> Mental pain is less dramatic than physical pain, but it is more common and also difficult to bear. The frequent attempt to conceal mental pain increases the burden: It is easier to say, "My tooth is aching" than to say, "My heart is broken."[3]

Do you see the trickery going on here? This is not what God wants for you. The enemy seeks to keeps you confined, captive, and stagnant. God wants you to be free of any charges against you. Don't think you don't possess the necessary resources to confront your issues. He has sent you the Holy Spirit. This means you have power to confront any issues that are keeping you from fulfilling your assignment. You have to stir up the Spirit of God in you and move in faith. Begin to apply the Word in your life.

> But you have received the Holy Spirit, and he lives within you.
> —1 JOHN 2:27, NLT

Hidden Pain

"If you want to be free, you are going to have to confront him," I told her, as she looked at me with tears in her eyes.

"I can't forgive him," she said. "He abused me for years. I can't face him."

I could not understand her pain. I had never experienced the horrors this woman had experienced as a child. He had robbed her of her innocence. This went on for years. Then one day she mustered up enough courage to pack a small bag, and with great fear of the unknown, she walked out, never to return. She tucked the horror away in a secret closet in her heart. She locked it securely, never to be opened again.

Fast-forward, and what do I see as the storyline of this woman's life? Two failed relationships, abuse, addiction, and suicide attempts. Although she had later surrendered her life to God, on this particular day this young, beautiful, professional woman sits in my office, broken and horrified by the childhood memories that have resurfaced.

To the naked eye she had it all together. Yet something was happening. As God was getting ready to promote her in ministry, something was unleashing in her heart. The internal closet doors she had locked so securely had swung wide open and displayed the horror of many years earlier.

God wanted her to confront her greatest pain. She needed to be completely free. God wanted to promote her and bless her beyond her wildest expectations.

Seven years earlier she had given her life to Christ. She thought she had forgiven her father. Yet one day while in prayer she was confronted with her pain. She realized she had not forgiven him. She convinced herself that he would not affect her future. She was going to release herself of him, yet he still controlled her emotions.

Her love for God was the driving force that took her to the hospital where her father lay as a patient. He was very ill. She was there to confront one of her biggest fears and forgive. She wasn't alone; God was with her through it all. She was convicted, she confronted, and she prevailed.

If God calls us to come face-to-face with our greatest fears and pains, He is going to be there with us. He will not leave us or forsake us. This is the assurance we have. Our job is to believe and trust God.

She looked into his eyes and, with tears in her eyes, said, "Dad, you sexually abused me, and it hurt me for a long, long time. But I am here to tell you that I forgive you."

She did it! She was released from the bondage of unforgiveness. Imagine the weight that came off her shoulders.

You can do it too. You have the power to forgive. Forgiving someone does not mean that you accept the wrong that was done. It means that the wrong done no longer has power over your life.

Today she is on assignment and fulfilling God's call over her life. Her horror became her testimony, and many have been transformed as a result. The sins of her father no longer have power over her life.

Learn to Let Go

Are you willing to let it go? Rid yourself of all that has hindered your progress? I contend, you ought to get to the root of your ailments. You need to extract the root so that a new seed of hope and restoration can grow. Until you confront those things that control your thoughts and your emotions, you will not be able to walk away and effectively fulfill your assignment. Everywhere you go your pain and unresolved issues will follow. Until you empty yourself, God cannot pour into you. What are those things you need to confront and let go?

- Past hurts
- Abuse
- Faulty thinking
- Bad eating habits

- Fear
- Unforgiveness
- Bitterness
- Betrayal

When matters like these stay inside your heart too long, they can become poison to the soul. They take root, and as they continue to grow inside, they become entangled with other internal activities. Before you know it, you are in a spiritual, physical, and emotional web of chaos.

As a matter of fact, we cannot genuinely enjoy blessings, open doors, provision, or opportunities unless there has been a cleansing of the soul. There were times when God would bless me in specific ways, but I could not enjoy the blessings because I was focused on some other mess going on in my life.

These are things we should not ignore. Every day we wake up, open our eyes, and sip our favorite drink is a God-moment and an opportunity to enjoy God's very best. Yet many of us fill it with worry and concerns over things God can handle. This is often the result of unresolved matters of the heart that must be confronted.

What are you willing to do to get to the place where God wants you to be? Are you willing to confront your issues?

There was a woman who had an issue of blood for twelve years. (See Luke 8:43–48.) This woman tried everything in an effort to get well. She had sought treatment and consulted doctors, all to no avail. I would imagine this woman was both physically and emotionally exhausted.

On one particular day her spirit was stirred. This woman was determined to come face-to-face with her issue and say, "Enough is enough." This was the day Jesus was in town. "If He did it for others, then He can do it for me," she may have thought. She came face-to-face with her fears, the crowd, and her circumstance. Reaching for Jesus, she came from behind and touched His cloak. Her touch caused Jesus to stop and say, "Someone touched me; I know that power has gone out from me" (Luke 8:46).

Falling at His feet in full surrender, she identified herself. She did not stop there. She confessed her ailment and described her issue. What great faith! She knew in her heart that "if only" she could touch Him, she would be made whole. Her faith had already healed her. Her unwavering determination to be "fit" in health, and knowing where to go, provided the miracle she needed. This woman let go of her issues at the feet of Jesus. She emptied herself out.

God wants us to let go of our issues as well. Leave them at His feet; He will know what to do with them. He wants our pain, habits, faulty thinking, bitterness, unforgiveness, anger, shame, guilt, and any other unhealthy ailment. We should not allow anything to hinder our progress. God wants to use us with power and might. As He was with Joseph, He wants to be with us so that anything that we set our minds and hearts to do will prosper.

I hope that I have given you enough evidence to embrace confrontation as something good rather than something you want to run from. I am not suggesting that it is easy to confront, but you may find that as you embrace it, it is not as difficult as you thought it would be.

Let me remind you of something you need to remember: You are not alone. God will give you the courage, the power, and His Word. The moment you confront and let go, you create a void that God will fill with a new revelation for your life. There are things God wants you to know, and He is ready to reveal them to you.

Get ready for step 3, as you receive the revelation.

A Post From the Fit for Your Assignment Facebook Group

What a day! I shared with someone today how good I was at ignoring certain things…But since this whole challenge thing—which is the reason why I stopped journaling for a while, too much comes out—I have been convicted and confronted. I found out confrontation causes us to fight, [to] go against the current. Conviction and confrontation, wow! I've asked God, why? Well, I was told I am in the Potter's hand. Maybe God took the clay jar (me), put it to the light, and said, "Wait, there is a smudge. Let's start over." So true! Where I am going, where my family is going, God won't allow those smudges to remain. There are things stagnating me and that is not what I am called for. Does it hurt? Yes, but I am growing.

⇒ *Reflections* ⇐

When we come face-to-face with our pain and struggles, God is right there with us.

1. Can you think of a time when you confronted something and felt the peace of God immediately after?

_____

_____

_____

_____

_____

_____

2. Are you willing to write about some issues or past hurts that you know God is asking you to let go of so that healing can take place?

_____

_____

_____

_____

_____

_____

Chapter 9

STEP 3: REVELATION

Whether you turn to the right or to the left, your ears will hear a voice behind you, saying, "This is the way; walk in it."

« ISAIAH 30:21 »

Revelation: "An act of revealing to view or making known," or "something that is revealed by God to humans."[1]

FOR A SEASON in my life I moved to my own rhythm. I was often misaligned, either behind or ahead of God. I attribute this to being overworked and emotionally exhausted in ministry. OK, some of it I should attribute to stubbornness as well. I was in survival mode. It wasn't a good place to be. I had some difficult moments. The truth is, there were days I simply wanted to make it through the day. You do know what I mean by that, right? The "let's just make it through this day" kind of day? I became very good at internalizing my pain so that I could survive while on my assignment.

On one occasion I woke up with a pain in my abdomen. I thought it was something I had eaten, and it would go away. As the days passed, the pain grew worse. After weeks of excruciating pain, I made my way to the doctor's office, where a medical test and ultrasound was conducted. I was certainly not ready for what happened next.

I received a call on my cell phone from a friend who worked at my doctor's office. I knew something was wrong as she proceeded to ask, "Is Charles with you?" Charles is my husband, and he was not with me at that moment. What reason would there be to ask a grown woman if her husband was with her? With great apprehension she told me that the ultrasound revealed an enlarged pancreas, and I needed to be hospitalized immediately. The doctors felt it was a life-threatening circumstance.

Her voice continued to echo in my mind. I thought for certain it was a mistake. I was determined to be strong for everyone. I didn't want my husband or my family to worry.

I was admitted that night to the oncology floor. My husband would not leave my side, and my father ran to his prayer room. That evening in the hospital I became very sick. I was too sick to really absorb what was happening. Everything was happening so fast.

The next morning when I woke up, I battled with all that was happening. Why was God allowing this to happen to me? There was much to be accomplished. What happened to all the promises? They had yet to be fulfilled. Who would care for my family? I wondered if I had done all God had wanted me to do. Was this my time? Was it too late? I had not finished my assignments here on Earth. All these questions and more flooded my mind.

I woke up yet another morning to realize again I was not dreaming. I was really in a hospital. More concerning, I was on the oncology floor. My spirit was uneasy. "I do not belong here," I told myself over and over again. Something wasn't right.

Have you ever felt paralyzed by events in life? Sickness exists. Cancer exists. Loss exists. Yet we often convince ourselves that these events will never happen to us. Then one day there we are, face-to-face with our own mortality.

The doctor made his way to my bed, then sat near me and proceeded to tell me what was going to happen next. They were putting me through all sorts of exams. The word *cancer* was mentioned.

I could not believe what I was hearing. It felt like a tornado had picked me up and I'd landed in a place of utter chaos and uncertainty. "Oh, Lord, why?" I exclaimed. "My girls, my family; it's not fair. I am a pastor!" It felt like a nightmare. None of it made sense. The spirit within wanted to tell me something.

One day the doctor had finished his exams and was walking out the door, when without warning he made an abrupt stop. He turned around, and with an intense look in his eyes, he asked, "Are you a pastor?"

I told him indeed I was.

He paused, looked at me intently, and said, "Well, then, what are you waiting for? Start praying." I was stunned. Those words pierced me at the core. The moment I heard those words, I knew something spiritual had just taken place. My spirit leaped. The room, which felt cold, dreary, and depressing, lit up as I opened up my mouth and declared, "I do not have pancreatitis! I am going to live! I am leaving this hospital today! I am healed!"

Three hours later, after all the tests had been conducted, the doctor came in looking puzzled. He told me he could not understand what had just occurred. He asserted that the patient he checked last night could not possibly be the same patient. The new results had come back normal. In addition, the pancreas had returned to its normal size. I went home that evening. God had been with me every step of the way. The promises were still mine to take hold of. My assignment wasn't over.

I had just experienced God as He had revealed His power. I had become sick. I had contributed to my illness by internalizing my issues. Moreover, I had spent a period of time in spiritual slumber. God showed up at the right time. Not only did He reveal Himself to me by demonstrating that He is forever faithful, but He also revealed the power and authority bestowed upon me to confront my illness and declare healing over my body.

I learned that:

- Life happens, and we must be prepared for all circumstances.

- Negative circumstances and pain are opportunities for God to demonstrate His power.

- We have been given power and authority.

- God never leaves us or forsakes us.

- Our greatest revelation of God is often revealed in the midst of pain. It is in our pain that we become vulnerable. It is here that we recognize we are not self-sufficient but dependent on our God and Creator.

I was not taking care of myself as I should have. My body crashed. You see, self-care is important to God. If it is important to God, then it should be important to us. Emotionally I was a mess. Spiritually I was weak. And physically I was certainly showing it. Did I love *me* enough to be a good steward of myself? Let's see. I was not focused on me. I was so focused on everything else that I had neglected very important areas in my life. I realized that my life had to represent the God I served.

I had taken on too much responsibility. I wanted to manage it all. As a consequence, I faced high levels of stress. Stress, in my mind, was permission to eat whatever I wanted, whenever I wanted. It was therapy. It was delicious, tasty, and satisfying to the palate. Nothing felt so wonderful as indulging in my favorite comfort food.

I had chosen to take care of my health my way. Why would I want to talk to God about what I should be eating every day? Aren't there more important things to pray about? At least this is what I thought. I had convinced myself that God was not involved in my eating rituals. As long as I did not fry my food and I stayed away from sweets and refrained from eating after six, I was being a good administrator of my body. Please don't judge me. God was dealing with me; I just didn't know it yet.

I am not an expert in nutrition, but I know that I had a stinky mentality as it pertained to eating. The enemy wanted me to believe that there were areas in my life where I did not want God to get involved.

"Reina, go ahead, have that big plate of starch right before you preach," he'd say. "No worries. You'll burn those calories in no time."

I remember one time in particular when I ate terribly wrong before a speaking engagement. Boy, did I have to pray my way through the message. I felt faint and weak. Let's be honest, who could resist a delicious plate of comfort food when feeling famished? Why couldn't I be like Jesus, when He addressed Satan, "Thou shalt not tempt the Lord thy God" (Luke 4:12, KJV)? Instead, without hesitation, I indulged in absolute pleasure, as my flesh rejoiced and my spirit mourned.

Feeling quite full, weak, and sleepy, I took the platform and began to speak on the message I had prepared. Conviction came like an arrow piercing my heart. The moment I introduced my first point—self-control—I could hear God saying, "Reina, you are going to speak about self-control when your eating habits and so many other things are out of control?"

Yikes! Making every attempt to keep the message going without the audience noticing the hand of conviction upon me, I did what anyone with fear of the Lord and discernment would do. I brought that point to an end and moved on to the next topic.

I realized I was more eager to satisfy my flesh than satisfy my spirit. The truth is, I was not as hungry for His presence as I should have been. I had indulged in my wants, and the needs of my soul had not been met. I needed to hunger and thirst for God.

To be hungry for God is to long for righteousness. It is a deep, desperate desire to do right in His sight. It is having a heart pleasing unto Him. Those who thirst and hunger for God have a craving to be in His presence. Permanence in His presence satisfies our soul. To hunger and thirst after God is just as the psalmist cried out, "As the deer pants for flowing streams, so pants my soul for you, O God. My soul thirsts for God, for the living God" (Ps. 42:1–2, ESV).

In His presence we enter into alignment. We are endowed with the desire to please God; hence, in obedience we move toward His plan for our lives. We have been created to hunger for God. Many have searched high and low to satisfy their hunger with earthly commodities, yet they are never satisfied. Only God can satisfy the deepest need of the soul. (See John 6:27–35.) Scripture declares, "I am the bread of life; whoever comes to me shall not hunger, and whoever believes in me shall never thirst" (v. 35, ESV).

Every morning we wake up, we should ask God, "Give us this day our daily bread" (Matt. 6:11, ESV). In asking this, we are declaring that we are not self-sufficient; we are dependent on Him for our very survival. In asking God to give us our daily bread, we declare that He alone can sustain us. Can you imagine what would happen if every morning we prayed this prayer, knowing that His Word cultivates our mind, will, and emotions? There must be recognition on our part that we need Him every day, as "his mercies never come to an end; they are new every morning" (Lam. 3:22–23, ESV).

As I preached that sermon after showing no sense of self-control over what I ate and conviction weighed heavily upon my spirit, it was not God's desire to beat me down and make me feel unworthy. Quite the contrary; He wanted to awaken in me a desire to care for myself so that I could experience more. I had to make the changes. I had to get rid of the old habits and pick up new ones. I needed direction, strength, and accountability. I began to seek His presence relentlessly! I was determined that I was not going back. I was so excited that I began to share with others what God was doing with me.

The Fit for Your Assignment Revelation

I was sitting in my office ready to turn on my computer one day, when I clearly heard, "Fit for My assignment." I recognized that those four words were saturated with God's presence and asked, "What, Lord?"

He responded, "That is what I want you to name the group on Facebook—Fit for My Assignment."

I heeded His voice, and without hesitation I opened a private group page. It would be a place where I could make myself accountable. Within minutes of hearing His voice, my spirit was stirred as I received with such clarity, for the first time, a revelation pertaining to my next phase in ministry. My life was about to take another turn for the better.

Are you following the pattern yet? Where there has not been conviction, confrontation was not present, and there was seldom a fresh revelation until there has been confrontation. As the adage goes, "You cannot put the cart before the horse." God is a God of order. And to help us avoid injury, He takes us through the proper processes so that when we are basking in the fruit of our labor, we don't get interrupted because we have missed a step.

I had yearned for a revelation. In so many occasions I pleaded with God to show me a glimpse of what the future held. For years He was silent. I had surrendered to the fact that maybe the best had already come and gone. But why was I yearning for more? Was it because I recognized I was a carrier of His glory?

Despite my shortcomings I could feel the weight of my assignment. There were so many moments of mental chaos, where I didn't know what God wanted for me. Yet God was faithful. He was silent for a season but always remained faithful.

As I sat in my office, God began to speak to my spirit. I had been convicted and confronted, and now God was speaking: "You have arrived. You are where I want you to be."

I knew what He meant. He did not need to explain. I was not at the top of a pyramid or at the peak of my ministry. No; I was at the right place in my journey with God. I knew what He meant, and it was soothing to my soul. Along with the word came the revelation. I had been obedient. Obedience made room for my promotion. I had aligned some areas in my life, and as a result I understood what He had wanted to teach me all along. He wanted me to desire Him more than anything else. He wanted me to have total dependence on Him. He wanted to help me change areas in my life that were falling apart. When I decided I was going to become spiritually fit above all else, He broke His silence.

The Value in God's Silence

God's silence doesn't mean He has abandoned you. Let me ask you something: Has God been silent in certain situations in your life, causing you to wonder if He was there? This is one sure way to doubt God—or worse, doubt His existence. Your mind conjures up its own conclusions: "There is no God. If there was, He would care." "He doesn't care." "If there is a God, then I'm just not good enough for Him." Don't give in to the lies of the enemy. We all go through these mental battles, but through it all, hold on to Him. He will speak.

There was a time in my life when I really wanted God to speak to me. I wanted Him to fight my battles. The people I loved and considered friends had hurt me. My heart was broken. I was at a loss for words. I spent days in silence with a broken heart. I remember becoming really angry. When I finally broke my silence, I said, "OK, God, I guess I deserved this. I don't expect You to help me." I confess; it was a poor attempt to get God to break *His* silence. It didn't work. Through it all He sustained me. God is always near to the brokenhearted.

Guilt and shame often keep us from running to God, yet there isn't anything that can keep God away from us. He wants nothing more than for us to run to Him in those times when we feel unworthy. Scripture declares, "Then you will know that I am in Israel, that I am the LORD your God, and that there is no other; never again will my people be shamed" (Joel 2:27).

Everything that God does is orchestrated, even His silence during some of our darkest seasons. In John 11:1–37 we find two sisters grieving the death of their brother, Lazarus. It is important to understand that prior to his death, the sisters sent notice to the Lord that Lazarus, the one He loved, was sick (v. 3). When Jesus heard this, He responded, "This sickness is not unto death, but for the glory of God, that the Son of God may be glorified through it" (v. 4, NKJV). Jesus then waited two more days before He went to visit the sisters. The sisters must have been devastated as Jesus was silent. Yet when Jesus arrived, He spoke the word and Lazarus was raised from the dead.

Yes, silence often means that God is working something out behind the scenes in your favor. He will be glorified. Your mess will become a message; your test will become your testimony.

You can be assured that God's silence has purpose. Not only is He getting ready to glorify Himself in your life, but He is also inviting you to trust Him. Yes, trust Him even when you can't hear Him or feel Him. It is during these times that you must be still and know that He is God (Ps. 46:10). Let me encourage you: God always arrives on time. His timing is perfect, and His silence is about to reveal His glory even in your darkest of circumstances.

You are God's most precious possession. Don't allow the enemy to convince you into thinking you are not good enough. You are more than good; you are amazing. You are so amazing that God is always thinking about you. The Word of God says that every single day you live is recorded in His book (Ps. 139:16).

The reason He deals with your heart is because He wants you to discover the treasures He has carefully placed inside of you. He doesn't want you to dwell in the past. He wants you to look ahead. Can you hear Him as He says, "Do not remember the former things, nor consider the things of old. Behold, I will do a new thing, now it shall spring forth; shall you not know it?" (Isa. 43:18–19, NKJV). Unlike things, people, and places, God never leaves a void in your heart. He replaces the old with the new. This is how God works.

No More Voids

When I think of the word *void*, I envision an empty space where the only thing that exists is the void itself. A void has its residence in the heart and soul of humanity, yet our hearts and souls desire wholeness. It is here that our struggles begin. Our hearts and souls yearn for meaning, relationship, and worth. I have seen too many people attempt to fill their void with meaningless pleasures and temporal possessions.

The only way to satisfy any longing and hunger is to possess an understanding of what it is that we hunger and long for. So let me ask you: What do you truly hunger for? Is there a longing in your soul that has yet to be satisfied? A void that hasn't been filled? A deep desire beyond the range of human comprehension? What if I told you that God has placed in us a void that can only be filled by Him? It is a place created to house His presence and satisfy your hunger.

The Lord will not just come in and fill us. According to Revelation 3:20 (ESV) He must be invited:

> Behold, I stand at the door, and knock. If anyone hears my voice and opens the door, I will come in to him and eat with him, and he with me.

Filling the void of our hearts is our choice and His desire. He longs for a relationship with us, yet we must be awakened to the acknowledgment that only the Lord can bring meaning to a meaningless life and satisfy the deepest hunger.

I will never forget the first time she led me to her secluded place. No one had ever been invited there, not even those closest to her. How we got there is vague in my memory, yet I clearly remember the warmth and coziness of the room. I remember the smell of fresh brewed coffee and the smile on her face as we shared stories of our life journey. One minute we were sitting in her living room, where vibrant colors coupled with her personality painted a portrait of a woman who reflected exuberance and passion; in the next minute we had transcended to a dark, cold, empty space in her life.

She had been a victim of emotional abuse most of her life. It started with her parents. When she left her home to live with the man she believed to be the love of her life, she endured more emotional and at times physical abuse. During her early teenage years she became an alcoholic. She would seclude herself in her room and drink her pain away. She told me she felt empty most of her life. She had settled and believed that this was her life, and she just had to accept it. She was led to believe that she had to embrace all that life brought her way. Religion had taught her that this was her punishment for sinning and getting pregnant at a very young age.

Who was she to demand that God change her circumstances? Her heart had grown cold.

She had a void in her heart, an emptiness that kept her bound in shackles of depression. She never felt loved. She spent most of her childhood and teenage years seeking acceptance from her parents. She finally gave up, and at the tender age of fourteen she left her home to be with a young man she believed would give her all the love she needed. She was sure that this young man would give meaning to her life. She was mistaken; her relationship took her deeper in pain and landed her in an abyss of depression. Looking to numb her pain, she turned to alcohol, affairs, and food.

One day she received a knock on her door. A childhood friend whom she had not seen in years had stopped by to invite her to church. She accepted the invitation not expecting anything.

She was cordial as she made her way through the doors of the small church. It had been so long since she had attended a church service. She proceeded to walk in and sit in the back of the church.

She enjoyed the worship and the warmth of the people. When the orator began to speak, the atmosphere changed. It became very personal. She couldn't believe what she was hearing. She wondered how the orator knew of her life; she had not shared it with anyone. She felt someone at the door of her heart. It had been a long time since she felt that someone cared. God was knocking gently yet persistently. She had a choice to make: Would she let Him in? What would this mean? God could not possibly love her after all she had done to herself, she thought. Yet she made her way to the altar and said, "Yes, Lord, come into my heart."

Let me tell you what transpired as a result of her decision to accept the Lord's invitation into her empty heart. Although her external circumstances remained the same for a period of time, her life changed internally, and as a consequence she was now fit to move in the life God had assigned for her. She became endowed with peace instead of chaos, joy instead of sadness, love instead of anger, and self-control rather than loss of control. Today she is free of abuse and on assignment. She leads a ministry and has a passion for God that causes others to follow suit.

God will never walk into our heart and leave it empty. For every area that has been emptied out, God has a replacement. If God removes pain, He replaces it with peace. If He removes bitterness, then He replaces it with joy. If He removes unhealthy habits, He replaces them with new habits. You get the point.

God will never leave a void! One of God's greatest revelations for our lives is that He restores our voids so that every day we can be in full relationship with Him. He restores us so that there is a daily desire to meet, seek, and want Him passionately and relentlessly.

As we begin to pursue the eternal things, we realize that pursuing the things of this world can merely satisfy us temporally, but an eternal pursuit keeps our soul satisfied. C. S. Lewis wrote, "We are full of yearnings, sometimes shy and sometimes passionate, that point us beyond the things of earth to the ultimate reality of God."[2]

After we are exposed to the understanding that God is our source of meaning and purpose, we begin to walk in absolute authority in the Word of God. We are inspired each day to pursue a deeper revelation of God's intention for us. Moreover, we walk in our assignment with great confidence. We acknowledge that it is not by our means that we overcome, but by the power of God that is in us.

The most exciting step is just a couple pages away. Once our eyes are open to the revelation of who God is and who we are in Him, we are transformed in all areas of our lives. Are you ready for a metamorphosis? Let's go in together.

A Post From the Fit for Your Assignment Facebook Group

There are times when we have to look at the enemy straight on and tell him, "You have no power over me!" And then show him.

⇒ *Reflections* ⇐

God's silence doesn't mean He has abandoned you.

1. What does it mean to you to hunger and thirst for the presence of God?

_____

_____

_____

_____

_____

_____

_____

2. What are some things God has revealed to you in this chapter?

_____

_____

_____

_____

_____

_____

_____

Chapter 10

STEP 4: TRANSFORMATION

Create in me a clean heart, O God, and renew a right spirit within me. Cast me not away from your presence, and take not your Holy Spirit from me. Restore to me the joy of your salvation, and uphold me with a willing spirit.

« PSALM 51:10–12, ESV »

Transformation: "Change in form, appearance, nature, or character."[1]

P ASTOR REINA, THERE is something different about you." I heard these words, and I knew something had changed. This woman who greeted me after church may not have known what about me had changed, but I knew. I had gone through a spiritual metamorphosis. I had gone through conviction and confrontation, had received a revelation, and now transformation was inevitable. I had a newfound passion for God, ministry, and life. The God I had served for so many years had complete dominion over my life. I had surrendered wholeheartedly to His pursuit over my whole entire heart.

Everything I needed I found in His presence as I came face-to-face with the very essence of who God was in my life.

God had created a new heart and renewed a right spirit within me, which launched me toward my assignment with a new and improved attitude. Don't be fooled, however; my transformation did not just happen. I had to be honest with myself and with God. I even had to make some confessions along the way.

It is difficult to live life pretending to have it all together, only to come home and have to deal with the real self. I would often say to myself, "Reina, how long do you think you can keep this going?" I was referring to walking in my assignment yet being tired and stagnant in so many areas.

What we often do not realize is that we can be engaged in ministry or work and not be satisfied. If we are not nurturing our soul with the Word of God and with a time of conversation with Him that goes beyond a "give me" prayer, we can become weary. If we are not placing the pause button on ministry long enough to allow the wind of the Spirit of God to refresh and replenish our souls, we will grow weary and spiritually weak.

Ministry had become a burden too heavy for me to carry, so I did what people who are not fit do: I justified my inability to take time to strengthen my spiritual stamina. It was kind of how I had approached exercise. The thought of exercising was exhausting, and for the most part, I justified my lack of exercise with being too busy.

I couldn't understand my husband's enthusiasm when he first received his INSANITY workout videos. Well, his enthusiasm was so contagious that I decided I was going to try it myself. Why not? "How hard could it be?" I thought. Besides, I thought that taking the time to exercise with my husband would be an added benefit to our already wonderful marriage. You would think the title INSANITY would deter me from moving into such unfamiliar territory. But no!

Well, let's just say that when I was done with day one of this video, it confirmed my relationship with exercise—I never had one! Physically I was hurting. Every part of my body cried, "Help!" I had convinced myself that I could do this without preparing my body. The difference between my husband and me was that he often exercised and I didn't. His body was prepared for the leaps and bounds of this video. He stretched his muscles often to prevent injuries, as he was accustomed to playing racquetball and working out.

It dawned on me, after the fact, why my husband often felt it necessary to tell me, "Reina, you need to stretch before you work out. You need to get your body ready and your muscles loosened."

I usually responded, "I'll stretch *while* I work out."

Yeah, sometimes husbands do know best! He would tell me that stretching and warming up would lead to optimal performance and less injuries. But would I listen? Of course not.

Here is the correlation: God wants us to be in optimal spiritual shape so that we can do and be our very best. I have to confess there were some assignments in my past that I should have done better. God had provided all I needed; I had chosen, however, to jump into these mindlessly. I just wanted to get them done and move on. Doing this kept me blind to understanding God's vision. There were plenty of times I was injured while on assignment. I realize now that many of those injuries could have been prevented had I taken the time to prepare accordingly.

My exercise fiasco with the INSANITY video was congruent with my approach toward spiritual fitness. I cannot believe I survived some of my assignments without preparation. I may have survived them, but let me be honest, I felt the aftermath of going in unprepared. But God was forever gracious. He waited patiently and then said, "Are you done yet? Because I can't wait to get started." I had convinced myself that I was ready for anything life would bring. I quickly found out this was far from the truth.

God wants us to prepare and train for the assignment before us. He too wants us to warm up our spiritual muscles in preparation for the task ahead. This is why God desires for us to be in relationship with Him. He wants to speak to us, prepare us, stretch us, and align us for the task. Through prayer, times of meditation, and reading the Word we build resistance and muscle endurance. I thought that I could get away with my lack of training and preparation and quickly jump into the task. Injury awaited.

We are not called to simply go *through* life. We must *prepare* for life if we are going to live life at our fittest. This may be contrary to what some of us have been taught. It is often said that there are things for which we cannot possibly prepare.

While there are things we may not be ready to confront, such as the loss of a loved one or a job, or the end of a relationship, God does tell us that there is a time for every season under the sun. (See Ecclesiastes 3.) We may not know how we are going to react in certain seasons of our lives. Yet we know that these seasons are inevitable.

How we endure and how we end up on the other side—spiritually, emotionally, and physically—are dependent on how fit we are in these areas when circumstances present themselves. This is why God transforms us. He changes our thinking, priorities, and self-sufficient attitudes by aligning our hearts and connecting our earthly vessels (self) to His divine sovereignty.

Running on Empty

One of the hardest things I had to do as a pastor was to tell three little children that their mother had passed away. They went to bed one evening and woke up to a woman they hardly knew (me) sitting before them, telling them that while they slept, their mommy had passed away.

I knew this woman who had died in a tragic car accident. We had grown up together. Her sister was a member of our church. I watched as a family cried out inconsolably for someone they were not prepared to lose.

This had happened early in my ministry. I had to depend on God for strength and words of wisdom. Did I feel I was ready to handle it? It wasn't until I was in the trenches of the ordeal that I realized God had been preparing me to walk in this particular assignment. My spirit was aligned. I had been praying, seeking

God for direction in all areas of my life. I was very dependent on Him because ministry was new to me.

I walked with this family for weeks as they transitioned to their new "normal." I often endured late hours hearing the cries of children and sisters as they grieved and mourned the loss of their loved one. My faith was steady. I was able to serve this family in time of great need without feeling depleted. This was possible only because seated at the throne of my heart was God. He led me, all the way.

Fast-forward many years later. Another beautiful young lady from our congregation went to be with the Lord, and I found myself depleted, tired, and questioning God. How could this happen? This young lady loved God. She loved life. I watched as the family who loved her cried out in desperation as they too questioned God. The cry of an inconsolable child sobbing, "I want my mommy!" echoed through the walls of my home for weeks. These were echoes of a seven-year-old little girl who would never feel the embrace of the woman she called Mommy. It didn't seem fair.

My husband and I rallied around this family. As a church, we came together. We prayed with them, cried with them, and mourned their loss. Their pain was beyond our scope of understanding. *We* had lost a loving member of our congregation, but they had lost their mom, wife, friend, and daughter.

Emotionally I was depleted. I had questions, and my spirit was weak. Yes, this is how I felt. After I had given all of me, I was left empty and did not consider replenishing my soul. I had to keep going; there were things that needed to get done.

I fought with God, asking Him why He hadn't prepared me for this loss. Why couldn't He have alerted me to the fact that tragedy was about to happen? The death was sudden. It seemed so unfair. Prepare me? Alert me? How could He? Ministry was happening, and I was so busy working a growing church that I had neglected to take time to be still long enough to hear the voice God. As a matter of fact, my prayers became monologues as I routinely asked

God to give me, give me, and give me some more. Here I was, not realizing that God wanted to dialogue with me.

The difference between the first loss and this one was not the manner in which I cared for and ministered to the families; it was the manner in which I cared for and ministered to myself. The gap between the two had been years. I had poured myself out over the years, and I was empty. I had not spent time in God's presence as I should have. I had become so busy doing ministry that I thought "working" for God was enough.

I needed a transformation. I needed God to restore my joy. God was trying to get me to look at myself. He wanted to transform my thinking, rid me of my self-sufficient arrogance, and bring me back to His desire and purpose. He simply wanted me healthy.

Have you at times found yourself making all kinds of requests to God yet not sitting still long enough to hear His response? You miss what He wants to reveal to you. I am not asking you so that you could walk away feeling guilty; I am asking you because I too am guilty as charged of not sitting still long enough to hear God's response to my requests, without truly realizing what I was doing. More importantly, I want to stress that if we are not thirsty for God or do not feel the need to hear from Him, there is something wrong internally.

The psalmist cried out, "My soul thirsts for God, for the living God. When can I go and meet with God?" (Ps. 42:2). Can you hear the desperate longing of the soul—a soul longing to be refreshed by the awesome presence of God? It was a thirst so intense that the psalmist could not wait for the encounter with God. His soul was so parched and yearning so deep that his soul cried out in a desperate plea. Every dry bone, weary mind, heavy heart, and feeble body desired to be submerged in the very presence of God's unfailing love.

We have been created for a longing that only God can satisfy. It is when we are one with God and His plans and purposes, and have an understanding of His sovereignty, that our souls are satisfied.

A parched life ceases to dream for spiritual things. There isn't any spiritual movement or excitement. People often come to me and tell me they have lost their spiritual stamina. Life is not as exciting as it should be. This is when the enemy comes in. All of a sudden presented before you are earthly desires and pleasures enticing enough to make you want to leave your spiritual post, even if for a moment. The problem is that curiosity has caused some people to never return to their post because they totally lost sight of their assignment.

Let's stop here for a moment. Take a moment to check your spiritual vitality.

Put your name before the following questions and ask yourself:

- Do you hunger and thirst for His presence?
- Are you dreaming for greater things?
- Do you have a vision?
- Are you excited as you get up each morning?
- Can you feel God moving in *all* areas of your life?
- Do you have the energy to run that extra mile if you had to?
- Do you possess endurance to run the race?
- Do you have enough spiritual fuel to take you further on your assignment?
- Are you prepared for the unexpected seasons of life?

If you answered no to at least one of these questions, and you know the Holy Spirit is prompting you, then stop and pray this prayer:

Dear Lord,

I need You now. Forgive my busyness. Restore my joy and bring back the desire and passion for You. I want to hunger and thirst for Your presence. I long for Your touch and embrace. Meet me here, Lord, and make me

fit to move in all that You have for me. Thank You, Lord.
In Jesus's name, amen.

The way I see it, some things just cannot wait! Now you can keep reading with the assurance that you are experiencing your own transformation as you read on. Isn't God good? He is never late!

I Surrender All

I believe that some of our greatest transformations are an outcome of some of our most difficult trials. The process and journey that our spirit goes through build and make our feeble bones strong. It is often during our struggles that our greatest strengths are discovered. Why? Because it is in the valleys of life that we may have no other alternative but to depend on God to get us through whatever difficult circumstances we may be facing. Depending on God often means to surrender and being obedient despite the inner voice that wants to impulsively speak out in times of emotional chaos.

I had to surrender my thoughts, ideas, and opinions, and I had to trust that God had my best interest at heart. And why wouldn't He? Isn't He my Lord, my Creator? Yes, but there were times I would forget I needed Him.

We all can attest to this. Sometimes we think that just because we have a couple of victories in our pockets, we can now consider ourselves self-sufficient.

I know one thing for sure: I am all that I am because my identity is in Him. Whatever I have accomplished thus far—all the blessings, provisions, open doors, and favor—is simply a reflection of the God I serve.

How did I get here after this long journey? Obedience.

If we are going to be blessed in our assignments and see the fruit of our labor, we must obey. Obedience is being able to say yes to God's plan and then adhere to His rules rather than ours.

The Lord declares:

> If you fully obey the LORD your God and carefully follow all his commands I give you today, the LORD your God will set you high above all the nations on earth. All these blessings will come upon you and accompany you if you obey the LORD your God:
>
> You will be blessed in the city and blessed in the country. The fruit of your womb will be blessed, and the crops of your land and the young of your livestock—the calves of your herds and the lambs of your flocks. Your basket and your kneading trough will be blessed. You will be blessed when you come in and blessed when you go out.
>
> —DEUTERONOMY 28:1–6

So here is what God is saying: He declares that if you walk in obedience, not only are you blessed, but your children are also blessed. Everywhere you go, you are blessed. Is there anything wrong with blessings? I would say absolutely not; therefore, do not let anyone convince you otherwise. God loves to bless His children. He is our heavenly Father, and it is in His very nature to want to bless us.

When we walk in our assignment fit, focused, and dependent on Him, He desires nothing more than to pour down His blessings. When we walk in obedience and surrender to God, we are saying, "I am here, Lord. I trust You as I submit to Your plan for my life." God can now work from within us. Our hearts are open for complete transformation. Here is another confession: For years I had been asking God for very specific things. I knew that God had deposited something in my heart. I often went to God asking Him to provide the open doors of favor where He could use me. I wanted God to enlarge my territory.

But when conviction engulfed me and I confronted my reality, my request changed. I cried out to God, saying, "God, I repent. I humble myself before You, and I ask for nothing more than an intimate relationship with You!" In an instant my intentions became pure because they were about Him. I presented myself before God with a contrite heart, understanding that I had indeed neglected our relationship. I wanted nothing more than for God to restore what I had broken.

Today I yearn to be faithful in my relationship with God. In addition, I desire to live in daily dependency upon God for all the choices that I make. My hand is steady on the pulse of God as I seek to be reminded every day by the mere sound of His heartbeat and the depth of His love for me. Now God is opening doors I had only dreamed about.

You too can experience this transformation. The moment you are transformed, you will walk under a new vision, a new mind-set, a new perspective, and a new hunger that will catapult you into a life of complete victory. Am I saying you will be free from trials? Not at all. However, the manner in which you embrace them will change. Your surrender, trust, and dependence on God will allow access for the Holy Spirit to penetrate into the crevices of your inner being, deepening your relationship with God and giving you greater understanding of your assignment.

Cover Me, Lord. I'm Going In.

Do you envision yourself wanting more of God? Do you see yourself living in daily dependence on Him, knowing that you are not self-sufficient? If this is your desire, then you are ready to take possession of all God is getting ready to impart into you. You have made it this far. Through trials and errors, valleys and hills, and all kinds of seasons, you are here and alive for such a time as this!

No matter where you find yourself today and whatever your assignment is, don't quit. Maybe you are saying, "Reina, this worked for you, but my issues are deeper and greater." If you are holding this book, then you are already in the process of transformation. God has met you where you are. You are being stretched.

Some things may be holding you down. Whatever your

challenges—marital, financial, work, ministry, school, or personal and internal conflicts—don't give up.

It is time to rise up and be transformed by the power of God's Word over your life. The mere fact that you are still alive despite some things you have gone through says that God is not finished and your assignment is not complete.

Whatever wrong choices you've made or unhealthy habits and faulty thinking you may have, make up your mind to stop the madness! How do you stop the madness? Well, get to the root of it and pull it out. The external condition of your body may only be a reflection of the state of your heart. So get in there and ask God to excavate until the culprit is found.

Are you ready to proclaim your victory? Well, let's declare together:

> As of today, I walk fit for my assignment. My unhealthy habits are replaced with healthy habits—no more lack of self-control as I give God all control. My spirit, soul, and body are now spiritually aligned to God's plan. My emotions are stable, and my heart is steady. My spirit is stirred, and my soul says, "Yes, Lord!"

No matter what comes your way, you get back up and start over until you have completed your assignment and reached your destination!

Your TRANSFORMATION is here!

A Post From the Fit for Your
Assignment Facebook Group

You know, I'm usually my worst critic. I constantly remind myself that I am not where I need to be in "Fit for My Assignment." But today as I'm separating clothes, I look at the piles, and I notice that my gym clothes pile is my biggest pile of clothes. So I know this is crazy, but I started to cry, because a year and a half ago, I could barely function. I despised my life. I was 94 pounds overweight. I went every day with pain in my knees and my joints. Asthma inhalers were my best friends, and I consider my life now. This second wind that God has afforded me, and I have to bless God. Sure, I may not be where I need to be, but bless God, I'm not where I used

to be.

⇒ *Reflections* ⇐

Obedience is being able to say yes to God's plan for you.

1. Are there some areas that need transformation? Name them.

_____

_____

_____

_____

_____

_____

2. Write about some areas that you feel God is transforming since reading *Fit for Your Assignment*. Write about what you can do to align with God's plan for you.

_____

_____

_____

_____

_____

_____

SECTION THREE
FINISHING WELL

I**T'S SATURDAY MORNING.** The sun is shining, and the weather is perfect for catching up on some outdoor work I've been putting aside. With good intentions I set out to start my day and be productive. "I'll gather my thoughts over breakfast and then get to work," I think to myself.

As coffee brews, I think, "I'll make the bed and tidy up the room." While making the bed, I hear the coffee maker alert me that the coffee is ready. Coffee in hand, I think it will be a good idea to put the dishes my daughters had left in the sink in the dishwasher. I didn't want to become frustrated by a mess. After loading the dishwasher, I realize I have run out of dishwashing detergent. "I know. I'll run out and get something simple to cook tonight and pick up the detergent while I am at it," I say to myself.

On my way to the supermarket I think, "What am I doing? If I don't get to the home improvement store, I will waste my day and not accomplish my outdoor work. The dishwasher can wait. I can grab something to eat later." I set out to the home improvement store.

As I am walking into the store, my husband calls, "Honey, my meeting was canceled. What are you up to?" (He listens to my response.) "Great, I will meet you there," he adds enthusiastically. As we walk about, he says, "With such a beautiful day, we should really consider getting that patio furniture we have been talking about, but I think we should look someplace else to evaluate our options." I concur.

OK, let me stop here and cut to the ending: the bed never got made, I didn't eat breakfast, the dishes remained dirty, detergent was never bought, the outdoor work was never started, and there was no patio furniture to show for our diligent day of shopping. I feel frustrated and unaccomplished. While this story is mostly hypothetical, let me be honest: this is how many of my days, weeks, and even months have looked like.

It reminds me of Nehemiah's efforts to rebuild the ruined walls and broken gates of Jerusalem.

> So we built the wall and the whole wall was joined together to half its height, for the people had a mind to work....All of them [the enemies] conspired together to come and fight against Jerusalem and to cause a disturbance in it.
> —Nehemiah 4:6, 8, nas

Half-built walls. Halfway there. The work stops because opposition and discouragement set in.

Perhaps you set out with great intentions. The enemy, however, saw your enthusiasm and set out to stagnate your progress. Maybe your greatest enemy is you. What are you going to do? Will you give in? Will you abort your mission and your God-given assignment? Absolutely not! Like Nehemiah, I encourage you to fight. (See Nehemiah 4.) You will not fight with physical strength. Instead you will fight with spiritual fortitude—calling on the name Jesus, declaring the Word of God, and allowing the Holy Spirit to endue you with strength to finish what you've started.

Opposition will come. Distractions will arise. Doubt will attempt to stagnate you. Insecurity will show itself like a giant too great to defeat. But let me remind you, you are a child of the living God. You've come too far. Quitting is not an option! Your assignment belongs to you, and there is no one better than you more qualified to fulfill it. So "let's not get tired of doing what is good. At just the right time we will reap a harvest of blessing if we don't give up" (Gal. 6:9, nlt).

Chapter 11

FINISH WHAT YOU STARTED

So now finish doing it as well, so that your readiness in
desiring it may be matched by your completing it out
of what you have.

« 2 CORINTHIANS 8:11, ESV »

ARE YOU READY to finish what you started? It's time to look at
all assignments that were started, yet because life happened,
they remain unfinished. Before we move in that direction,
take a moment to take inventory of your life and ask yourself if you
have taken care of any unfinished matters of the heart.

Throughout this book we talked about the importance of confrontation, of getting to the heart of the matter and making right
choices. I only pray that I was able to encourage you to look deep
into those areas and find the courage to move forward by dealing
with the issues.

I have the type of personality that when things are in disarray,
I become ineffective and my heart becomes restless. Hence the
reason I remained immobile for a season in my life. I would also
say that the Holy Spirit does this to us as well. When there is chaos
in our hearts and minds, it becomes difficult to be effective in
what God requires from us, and our assignment is compromised.

As you approach your assignment, it is good to set things in
order—resources, time, and talents. Order in our lives is good.
Lack of order brings about confusion and chaos. Order says that
we have taken time to examine everything before us and dealt

with it. It says we placed it in its proper location. Order in our lives declares that we have invested time in paying attention to ourselves and to the things are important to us because they are important to God. Scripture declares, "Pay careful attention to yourselves and to all the flock, in which the Holy Spirit has made you overseers" (Acts 20:28, ESV).

Setting things in order so that you can clearly see what God has given you may take some work. The truth of the matter is, becoming *fit for our assignment* takes work. Hard work is part of the process. *Work* is not a bad word. My definition of work is "doing something in order to achieve something."

Unfinished work speaks of our character. It shows that we have not planned properly or have let poor time management, busyness, or lack of order control our results. Our unfinished work reveals how we operate our lives on a daily basis. Ultimately how we operate our lives becomes the signature of who we are. When we begin to leave behind those poor signatures of our characteristics (hyphen intended), we are inevitably declaring that our character lacks the integrity to do things and live life with an excellent spirit.

Our character speaks of who we are; it is a manifested description of our very nature. As mentioned earlier in the book, I suffered from procrastination. I must admit, sometimes I still battle with it. But now, because I am aware of it and have confronted it, when it sneaks in, I deal with it before it deals with me.

Among the various negative effects procrastination had on my life, it caused me to leave behind a trail of unfinished work. It caused a delay on my assignment. If I had a dream linked to my current ministry assignment, I would tell myself that I had plenty of time to see it materialize. If I had an assignment with a due date, I would normally wait until the last minute, convincing myself that finishing would take little time. In the meantime I would add to my to-do list. It wasn't before long that the once easy-to-tackle projects became mountains of impossibilities. As a result, I often felt restless, self-critical, frustrated, and agitated.

You see, the problem was never getting started. The problem was finishing what I had started. I realize now that unfinished work was a consequence of misalignment in other areas of my life. I created a mountain of unfinished assignments so high that it obstructed my view of God's great blessings. I was missing out on the discoveries that awaited me on the other side of my completed tasks.

Your assignment is your ticket to grand discoveries. Let me explain. God has placed gifts inside of you. Gifts are to be used. Gifts, talents, and abilities combined can launch you into greatness. There are doors of favor that have been waiting for you; however, it is not until you complete one assignment that you are exposed to your next assignment. Each assignment is a world of discovery about you as a child of God and God as your Creator. But this is where the enemy comes in: he doesn't want you to see how wonderful God has created you. The enemy doesn't want you to be victorious in life. He doesn't want you to discover the greatness of God over your life. So what does he do? He uses your own unattended earthly desires to stagnate you on your assignment.

There are earthly and fleshly monsters that tend to keep us from finishing what we have started. For example: DISTRACTIONS. A distraction is "something that serves as a diversion or entertainment. An interruption; an obstacle to concentration. Mental turmoil or madness."[1] Here is a list of some of the distractions that can serve to keep us from moving forward in our assignment:

- ◆ Problems
- ◆ Relationships
- ◆ Money
- ◆ Routine
- ◆ Work
- ◆ Materialism
- ◆ Fear
- ◆ Doubt

These are but a few. I am certain you can add to this list.

Distractions rob you of your effectiveness. You can't be effective if you are distracted. The enemy uses distraction to steal valuable time from you and make you miss God-moments of opportunity.

This must cease. I wonder, how many moments have we missed because we have been distracted by other things?

Distractions can rob us from being effective in our assignments as parents, spouses, and all other tasks before us. Once distracted, we lose sight of what is in front of us. Our minds are divided between the assignment and the distraction.

I am reminded of people who have allowed distraction to reign in their lives. Distraction has gone from visitor to permanent resident in their homes and hearts. Today they have mourned the loss of what once was. What once was is no more; it has been replaced with a broken marriage, dead ministry, loss of job, no peace of mind, or financial chaos. The loss has come as a consequence of distractions. Distraction is self wanting to have its way by indulging in earthly desires. It is our flesh crying out for temporary pleasures.

There were quite a few men in the Bible who were distracted and either saw their assignment delayed or died before their assignment was completed:

- ◆ Samson had an assignment, yet his flesh led him into the wrong hands, and he died while on assignment (Judg. 16).

- ◆ Moses was distracted by the complaining of rebellious people. He did not follow God's instructions to do what God had asked him to do. He disobeyed God and was not allowed to enter the Promised Land (Num. 20).

- ◆ Sarah got ahead of God and delayed her assignment to become a mother (Gen. 16).

How about you? Do you have any examples of how distraction has caused a delay on *your* assignment?

Be Anxious for Nothing—You Will Complete What You Have Started

This is a story about how God showed up just when I was ready to give up.

Once upon a time this girl right here took a portion of Scripture to a whole new level. The scripture read, "Study to show thyself approved unto God" (2 Tim. 2:15, KJV). I decided that I was going to take three graduate courses. I was excited. Eager to finish my graduate work, I was willing to do whatever it took. I knew part of my assignment was to be a professional counselor, and I knew God was pleased with me getting my master's degree in professional counseling.

Toward the end of the semester all deadlines had to be met. I had written so many papers that semester, I lost count. I averaged six papers a week of no less than twelve to fifteen pages each. Well, each class having its own grand finale, I was now assigned to write papers that were over twenty pages long for each individual class.

This would probably have been less difficult if I didn't have all the circumstances that kept me from staying completely fixed on this assignment. I had a family to take care of, a church at which to minister, and a plethora of other responsibilities.

Let me pause for a second and ask you, Have you ever felt that though the assignment was too big to handle, you knew you had to do it? Because this is how I felt; as difficult as the task seemed, I felt God wanted me to stay on this assignment. I truly believed that this assignment was going to open doors for other assignments.

On the week when all papers were due, I began to feel the pressure of the deadlines ahead. I recall coming home from speaking at our church. I wanted nothing more than to put on my pajamas and cozy up next to my family and spend the evening in absolute comfort until I fell asleep. My body wanted rest. There was one problem: my spirit was restless because there was an assignment that needed to be completed.

I just love that the Spirit alerts us to what we should and should not be doing. I have to tell you, there are things I just cannot get away with because God just won't let me go! Is this a bad thing? No, actually it is a wonderful thing. It only means that God loves me immensely and wants me to live the way He intended.

I conjured enough energy to transition and get myself into writing mode. It was about two in the morning when I heard the voice of distraction saying to me, "You are tired. You can't do this. It's too much. You should stop now. Feel the pain in your body? You can hardly remain sitting. Look at all you need to do. How are you going to finish it all?"

I could feel my body in pain. I felt sick to my stomach. My heart began to race. I felt as though I was about to have an anxiety attack. I could barely keep my eyes open.

I started to doubt my ability to finish. I began to cry. I was tired; I had been tired for weeks. I had been running with so much— ministry, home responsibilities, and school. I had not stopped. The enemy was attempting to use a moment of weakness as opportunity for war. I felt weak. My spirit felt weak, and my soul yearned for rest.

I stopped writing and wept quietly, as I did not want to awaken my family, nor did I want to show them that I couldn't handle this task. They believed me to be a strong woman. I could feel my heart racing as a sharp pain took over my left arm. "Oh, God, I can't do this, I can't do this."

Have you desperately cried out to God, "Lord, this assignment is too much to bear! I can't do this! This is as far as I am willing to go"? It's a difficult place to be. Here I was, days away from the deadline, and I was falling apart. Notice I was so close to fulfilling my assignment, and yet I couldn't get myself to rise up and finish. I needed a second wind. I needed the wind of the Holy Spirit to revive me and bring peace to an anxious soul.

As I sobbed, I felt as though the room was caving in on me, and each unfinished task rested on my shoulder like bricks too heavy to carry.

How do you think I came out of this? Let me tell you.

I sat there hopeless and crying. Yes, I did—God's child, God's chosen vessel whom He had trusted with an assignment. What I did not know was that something was occurring in the spirit realm. God was waiting on me. God was waiting for me to use the authority He had given me to change an atmosphere as well as the outlook of a circumstance. Angels were positioned to quiet the voices. They were waiting on my cue.

As soon as my soul cried, "Help," the Spirit of God responded, "Here I am." Then this word from God came to mind: "Be anxious for nothing, but in everything by prayer and supplication, with thanksgiving, let your requests be make known to God; and the peace of God, which surpasses all understanding, will guard your hearts and minds through Christ Jesus" (Phil. 4:6–7, NKJV). God's living Word came to soothe my anxious soul.

Why did I think that God would forsake me? I knew deep in my heart He wouldn't. However, as I became distracted by the impossibility of the assignment, the enemy took it upon himself to build on my anxiety and fear and cause the assignment to look humanly unachievable. But God *is* my strong tower. I leaned on His Word. The spirit man inside of me took the soul by the hand and said, "Come on, give me your concerns. I win!" As a result, my body took its rightful position as I straightened up in my chair, organized my thoughts, and declared, "I can do all things through Him who gives me strength" (Phil. 4:13).

It was time for God to speak: "Reina, you can do this! Don't stop here. Finish what you started. There is great purpose for your life." The Great Encourager was cheering me on.

I did it! I finished the assignment. The final grade on all papers? One hundred! The reward was wonderful, but it was the process that taught me the most.

Do you see how the enemy tried to keep me from getting to the finish line? He wanted to keep me from my assignment because he knew my assignment would draw me closer to God. He sensed that my assignment would ultimately impact people.

This is what I am trying to say to you: Your assignment will not always be easy. It may be hard and even impossible, but God has given you the resources to become fit for your assignment, and you ought to take advantage. He has provided His Word, His presence, and an aligned heart. You can't possibly fail. Trust me. You are going to do amazing in your assignment.

Don't Let the Size of the Assignment Scare You

If God has placed an assignment that you see as too big or intimidating, I want you to know one thing: if He chose you, then you are the person for the job! On that premise you ought to embrace and take hold of the assignment. As a matter of fact, when we study Scripture, all assignments given to great men and women were so big they required supernatural faith. Let us first consider what Jesus declared: "Very truly I tell you, whoever believes in me will do the works I have been doing, and they will do even greater things than these" (John 14:12–14, NIV).

This is your moment. If you are reading this book, I can tell you God is tugging at your spirit and telling you, "Rise up and walk in the assignment I have given you." You have been created to do great things—things that will not only build your faith, but will also build the faith of those around you.

Remember young David the shepherd boy? God had chosen and anointed him. David was made aware of the terror that the Philistines were imposing on the people of Israel. Because he was endowed with greatness, favor, and anointing, his spirit was stirred within him. So he decided he was going to do something about it. David was willing to confront the giant (1 Sam. 17).

I don't know about you, but if it had been me facing a monster of a giant like Goliath, I may have been inclined to run back to the sheep I had left behind. Thank God it was David and not me on that field that day.

Of course, there will always be critics who may doubt your abilities on the basis of your appearance. But rest assured that you have been preparing for this all your life. All other assignments and tasks were preparing you for this one.

David knew how to fight off the enemy. He had been doing it in the field while protecting his father's sheep. The difference was that this enemy was slightly larger; OK, much larger! David was determined. There had to be something inside of him that said, "You can do this. This is your assignment. You have been chosen for this."

David had been preparing, becoming *fit* to take care of a giant Philistine. God had provided both internal and external resources to combat anything that would get in the way of his assignment. Yet for his protection King Saul wanted to dress him for battle. What Saul neglected to understand was that David had already been fitted for his assignment. All it took was a sling and a nice, shiny, smooth stone to bring down the giant.

How did he do it? How was David able to take down a giant and fulfill his assignment?

- He was the man for the job, anointed and appointed.
- He had faith.
- He had been preparing for this most of his life.
- He knew the God of Israel.
- He was focused.
- He was a man after God's own heart.

The assignment may seem impossible from the perspective of others, but to those whom God has chosen to fulfill the assignment and whose hearts are aligned, it is not a matter of how big the assignment is as much as how big is their faith in the God who assigned them!

God wants to manifest His glory through us. As we move in our calling, fit and empowered, we are proclaiming the good news of God. In our dependency on God to fulfill the assignment, we are building a relationship with God that reveals His very essence.

With each assignment God wants to expose His love, His character, and all of who He is through us!

Our assignment draws us closer to God and draws those to whom we are assigned close to Him as well. His love is known and His essence radiates through our everyday living and obedience.

Isn't it exciting to know that we are in partnership with a great God, the Creator of the universe? Are you ready to move in your assignment? Are you willing to finish what you started? I hope and pray you say yes. I am certain that now is your season to embrace God's assignment for you. It is going to be difficult at times. But the God who chose you will be there, and His power will be made perfect in your weaknesses. Don't just get *through* your assignment; be your very best at your assignment. You are victorious because the God in you is a God of victory!

A Post From the Fit for Your Assignment Facebook Group

Little did I know that God had worked on me through the night. I woke up in a different realm, ready to conquer. I am ready to take it all back, and that includes my health.

⇒ *Reflections* ⇐

Unfinished work speaks of our character.

1. What has been the greatest challenge for you in regards to becoming fit for your assignment? What has gone unfinished in your life?

_____

_____

_____

_____

_____

_____

2. Write down what has changed in your life since you started reading this book. What has God shown you? What are you willing to do to become fit for your assignment?

_____

_____

_____

_____

_____

Chapter 12

THAT WAS THEN; THIS IS NOW!

Let all that I am praise the LORD; with my whole heart, I will praise his holy name. Let all that I am praise the LORD; may I never forget the good things he does for me. He forgives all my sins and heals all my diseases. He redeems me from death and crowns me with love and tender mercies. He fills my life with good things. My youth is renewed like the eagle's!

« PSALM 103:1–5, NLT »

WHAT A JOURNEY becoming fit for your assignment has been. Can I tell you that the book you are holding in your hands is a result of complete spiritual alignment and surrender to God? When God gave me the concept of *Fit for Your Assignment*, little did I know that it would be a message to be shared with so many wonderful people such as you. I just wanted to be right with God. I wanted a relationship more than I wanted anything else. I believe God wants that for many, as here I am sharing this message with you.

I will never forget the good things God has done and is still doing in my life. He healed the ailments of my heart and renewed my youth. My prayer is that this book has awakened a desire and a passion in you to change patterns and behaviors. God wants you to be fully effective in all aspects of your assignment. A fit and aligned spirit, soul, and body will cause you to embrace your assignment with power, fulfilling all that God has called you to do.

It is important for me to remind you that becoming fit was a four-step process: conviction, confrontation, transformation, and revelation.

Conviction

I became undone when conviction made its way to my heart. Don't be afraid. To become undone means that now God can do you over again, just like the clay in the potter's hand. Perhaps as you read this book you were exposed to areas in your life that needed changing. Maybe some areas were neglected, and God has called you into account. This only means one thing: God is making you fit for *your* assignment. Something now changes in your life. Don't be surprised if things from your distant past begin to surface. This too is good. It means that God is cleaning your heart, and these things will no longer be able to have a grasp on you. Conviction serves to remind you that the Holy Spirit is active in your life. There is activity in your heart, which means God is going to make sure your flesh does not overrule your spirit.

Remember when I said conviction is not condemnation? Well, let me reiterate: Conviction doesn't want you to walk with your head down, feeling guilty and condemned. Conviction is God reminding you that you were made for more. Conviction builds you up to *His* standards.

Confrontation

This may be a difficult step for many people, and I can certainly understand that. However, if we are going to fully walk in our assignment, we must come face-to-face with our issues. Was it easy for me? Not the first time, or the second. Maybe not even the third. But the more I did it, the easier it became and the more liberated I felt. Let me encourage you that God will be with you all the way while you are engaged in this area of confrontation. The moment you can identify those areas that have hindered your progress, growth, and assignment, you must confront them.

Don't be fooled. God doesn't define confrontation the same way the world defines it. The world may say, "This is what I am going to tell you, and it is what it is. Deal with it!" But God says, "I want you to take those areas of your life that have kept you from moving in your assignment and identify them so that you can let them go. Make peace with Me and walk in the fullness I provide for you."

Do you see the difference? One keeps you down; the other lifts you up.

Revelation

It is here that God will make the plan and purpose for your life known to you. His dreams, desires, and vision for your life will begin to become clear. If you are in alignment, you will understand that they are *your* dreams and *your* plans, as given to you by God. You begin to see with clarity God's purpose and destiny for your life. God will reveal your heart and His heart as they merge together to beat one heartbeat.

One of the greatest things that has occurred in my life after so many years of serving God is that now I can truly say I can feel His pulse, His heartbeat. I know when I make Him sad. I know when I make Him smile. I know when I am in alignment. There is a keen awareness and assurance of His presence in my life. This is priceless.

I encourage you to allow God to reveal Himself to you as you expose your heart to Him. He wants to give you so much. Will you surrender it all to Him? I pray you do, because I know that He desires nothing more than to be in relationship with His children.

Transformation

Well, all I can say is, welcome to the new normal. It allows you to see the *then* and *now*.

Unfocused, uninspired, unhealthy eating habits, faulty thinking, lack of revelation, overweight, feelings of disgust, doubtful, fearful, unstable, unsure, unfit...

THAT WAS THEN!

Focused, determined, inspired, healthy eating habits, sound mind, revelation, joyful, assured, courageous, stable, sure, and fit for your assignment...

THIS IS NOW!

Breakthrough happened, and here I am. Breakthrough happened, and here *you* are.

This does not mean we are perfect or that we are better than anyone else; it means that we needed God more than anything else and God met us at our greatest need because we carried a message—a message, an assignment, a gift from God that needed to be shared.

Inside of you is a gift, a talent, an assignment that must be fulfilled. Perhaps you are on assignment but have no passion. You are tired. Life has beaten you down. You don't know where to begin, let alone pick up the pieces.

Well, what can I tell you?

This is why you are holding this book. God already started working in your life. Don't you quit. Don't you give up. Rather, rise up and say, "I will be all that God has called me to be. I will do all that God has called me to do."

As a pastor, minister, and leader it was not easy to expose my laundry list, but it was necessary. I realize that there are many who are in the trenches of ministry dealing with some issues that they dare not share with others. If this is you, then let me encourage you: there is nothing more liberating than when we put our titles down and say, "God, I need You."

You hurt too. You are human. You have feelings and concerns

and insecurities. Rather than hide and allow the enemy to imprison you within the walls of your title, status, or position, confront yourself. Let God do a marvelous work as He delivers your soul so that you may be most effective and used for His glory.

There were plenty of times I had to speak on miracles when I was still waiting for mine. These are times when life and ministry become too difficult to carry and we question God—"Where are You? Why do You have me on this assignment?"

The enemy often used this against me. The enemy wanted me to doubt God as well as the assignment over my life. It wasn't until I aligned my heart to the heart of God that even questions such as these became irrelevant. I realized that despite what I was going through, God was still God. And God is always faithful. I learned to wait on God's timing. And may I say, God is always on time. Moreover, I learned that the Lord who called me will be faithful to provide all that I need in due season.

Lastly, God wants to glorify Himself through you. He wants to reveal Himself through you to the world around you. As you move in your assignment, know that your relationship with God will deepen as you begin to hunger and thirst for His presence. Your relationship will grow as deep will call unto deep.

Here is my prayer for you:

I pray you live the life God has destined for you.

I pray you move in the fullness of your assignment with power and might because you have been chosen and anointed.

I pray you enter into the best season of your life.

I pray you are reminded every day of God's providence over your life.

I pray you will hunger and thirst for God.

I pray conviction will awaken you.

I pray confrontation will release you.

I pray revelation will ignite you.

I pray transformation will become you.

God asks, "Do you want to be made wholly fit in all areas of your life?" You have a choice to make. It is all about choices.

Prayer to God

Lord, I come before You today, and I declare that You have given me an assignment that I must fulfill. Today I ask You to search me, Lord, and examine my heart. Bring healing, restoration, and transformation to the areas that have affected my ability to move victoriously in my assignment. I surrender to You, Lord. All that I am is Yours—my spirit, soul, and body belong to You. Forgive me for any wrong that I have done. May Your mercy and grace cover me.

You know the plans You have for me. I give You my will, and may Your will manifest itself in my life.

I commit to prepare my spirit, soul, and body for the assignment that You have placed in my hands. I die to self so that You may live in me. I want to hunger and thirst for Your presence. I want to know You and be in relationship with You. I will call on You in my hour of need, and I will not be moved by the circumstances of life. From this day forward I trust You with my life as I come before You with a contrite heart and a willing spirit to be all that You ordained for my life.

I am Yours, Lord, to be used by You.

Get ready to accelerate as you become—FIT FOR YOUR ASSIGNMENT.

A Post From the Fit for Your Assignment Facebook Group

God has been so good to me! I have grown so much this year. Spiritually, I have never been where I find myself right now. In the beginning of the year I asked God to take me to a new dimension with Him. I trusted Him through a grueling pruning. I suffered loss. I cried and had moments of doubt and questions, but I dared to walk in the supernatural! It's been absolutely worth it! I can't be quiet about it. If God can transform my life, He can definitely transform yours! God does His best work with the least of these! To men you may be a mess, but to God, you are His beautiful masterpiece.

⇒ *Reflections* ⇐

You are His beautiful masterpiece.

Write one thing you know about yourself for each category that reminds you that you are His beautiful masterpiece.

    1. Spirit

    2. Mind

    3. Body

Complete each sentence.

My assignment is _____

_____

_____

I am committed to take care of my spirit because _____

_____

_____

I am committed to take care of my mind because _____

_____

_____

I am committed to take care of my body because _____

_____

_____

SECTION FOUR
THE FIT FOR YOUR ASSIGNMENT
THIRTY-DAY CHALLENGE

I PRAY THAT AS you navigated through the pages of this book, your spirit was stirred and ignited with a greater passion to bring yourself into alignment with all that God has for you. I know all too well that it is not easy to walk away from habits and fixed mind-sets. I also know that it is difficult to break free from areas in our lives that have kept us from fulfilling our assignment. I want to help you.

I have developed a thirty-day challenge to help you get started on your journey to becoming wholly fit. Thirty days may not be enough to change everything, but it will certainly get you started and on your way. Thirty days will be sure to help break or make some patterns. I believe we all need a starting point. Some of us perhaps need a little push, a bit of motivation, a prayer, and an encouraging word. Hence, allow me to provide you with thirty days of reflection and refocus, thirty days of trying something new and getting rid of something old.

Are you ready?

For this thirty-day challenge you will need a journal so that you can write your journey and progress each day. Truth be told, this is not simply a thirty-day challenge; it is the beginning of lifelong changes that will take you into all that has been destined for you from the beginning of time.

Get ready to nurture your spirit, mind, and body. Keep in mind that you will be challenged in these areas every day. God desires complete alignment.

So get ready to get fit for your assignment!

Day 1

WRITE THE VISION!

And the LORD answered me: *"Write the vision;* make it plain on tablets, so he may run who reads it. For still the vision awaits its appointed time; it hastens to the end—it will not lie. If it seems slow, wait for it; it will surely come; it will not delay."

« HABAKKUK 2:2–3, ESV, EMPHASIS ADDED »

WE ALL NEED to have a plan, set goals, and write the vision. Today's challenge is just that. Let's get started.

CHALLENGE

1. Take time to be in solitude.

2. Find a cozy place that makes you feel safe and comfortable.

3. Write what you want to accomplish in the next thirty days as it aligns with God's assignment for your life.

4. Focus on the spiritual, mental, and physical aspects of your life as you write the goals.

5. Write one goal for each of these areas.

PRAYER

Dear God,

Show me the areas that need to change. I need You to walk alongside of me on this journey. As I write my goals, make the vision clear. Prepare my spirit, mind, and body to receive what is ahead. Amen.

START NOW!

Beloved, I pray that all may go well with you and that
you may be in good health, as it goes well with your
soul.

« 3 JOHN 2, ESV »

HERE IS THE reality of it all: God wants us healthy inside and
out, so it is important to get rid of some things that are not
all that healthy. Are you up for the challenge?

CHALLENGE

1. Make a list of distractions that keep you away from
   your quality time with God.

2. Get rid of as many of these distractions as you can.

3. Clear the clutter in your mind and today choose to
   trust God with all the burdens of your day (pray).

4. Go into your refrigerator and your pantry and get rid
   of anything and everything that is *not* healthy, and on
   your next grocery trip replace it with healthy options.
   Fill your refrigerator with fruits and vegetables (your
   body will thank you). Replace chips and sweets with
   popcorn, nuts, raisins, cranberries, granola bars...the
   options are endless. Replace white bread, white rice,
   and white pastas with whole-grain versions. Get rid
   of sodas and fill a pitcher with iced cold water. Add
   lemons, strawberries, and other fresh fruits to your
   water to create your own flavored water. With a little

creativity, the possibilities are endless. Always consult a doctor for dietary restrictions, and read the labels. Not everything that sells as "healthy" is necessarily healthy for you!

PRAYER

Dear God,

I trust You. As I commit to spend more time with You, help me remove all distractions. My health is in Your hands. I give You my thoughts and every burden that affects my soul. I choose today to live a healthy life inside and out. Give me the courage to stay consistent. I trust You, Lord. Amen.

Day 3

TAKE A SELAH MOMENT!

Come to me, all who labor and are heavy laden, and I will give you rest.

« MATTHEW 11:28, ESV »

CONSIDERING THE CHAOS of each day, it is important to find time to be still and replenish. Sitting in God's presence will do just that! This is a time to pause, meditate, and clear out the clutter of the day. A few minutes may be all it takes.

CHALLENGE

1. Set your alarm for five minutes (or more if you can).

2. Find a quiet place.

3. Make sure there aren't any distractions—*none!*

4. Place your feet on the floor—relaxed.

5. Place your hands on your lap facing down—very relaxed.

6. Breathe in slowly. Breathe out very slowly. Feel your chest and body relax. Do this three times.

7. Clear your mind of any thoughts. Get lost in the moment of silence.

8. Invite God to invade your silence.

9. Be still and allow the Spirit of God to replenish your soul.

10. I challenge you to stay consistent with this exercise for thirty days.

Prayer

Dear God,

Today I trust that as I sit in silence, Your presence will cover me with love, peace, comfort, renewal, and restoration. I know that I can find rest in Your presence. Amen.

Day 4

THE DAY HAS ARRIVED—"E" DAY!

But I discipline my body and keep it under control, lest
after preaching to others I myself should be disqualified.

« 1 CORINTHIANS 9:27, ESV »

YOU REALLY DIDN'T think we were going to go through a thirty-day challenge and not incorporate exercise, did you? Remove all fear. This is a slow progression, and every move counts.

CHALLENGE

Before you start any form of exercise, consult your doctor so you can be sure of your limitations.

1. Set a fitness goal for the next twenty-six days, whether it is to lose weight, gain strength, or simply feel good and energized.

2. Log your plan on a calendar, giving yourself two days in between each day of exercise for rest and recovery.

3. Find a routine you will enjoy, and include variety so that you are not easily bored.

4. Start slow and steady. Fifteen to thirty minutes a day may be a great start if this is something new to you.

5. This is not a competition; go at your own pace.

6. Include cardio and strength training.

7. Start now! Try a fifteen-minute walk or run.

8. Keep your plan and your calendar where you can look at it every day. If you miss a day, don't beat yourself up, and do not give up! Start over tomorrow! Just don't make missing days a habit, because that too will become a habit.

PRAYER

Dear God,

As I prepare my temple to become wholly fit, provide the strength and zeal to boldly embrace this challenge. I trust that Your hand is always upon me and that I am more than a conqueror. I embrace this challenge. Cover me, Lord. I am going in. Amen.

WAIT. STOP. WHAT ARE YOU EATING NOW?

And God said, "Behold, I have given you every plant yielding seed that is on the face of all the earth, and every tree with seed in its fruit. You shall have them for food."

« GENESIS 1:29, ESV »

HERE IS A bit of truth: eating greens *does* keep you lean! The time has come to make some food changes. Again, this is not an overnight miracle. For some of you, like me, this is going to be a personal war! But I know you can do it. I did.

CHALLENGE

1. Add whole grains, fruits, vegetables, lean meats, and lots of water to your diet!

2. Get rid of the sodas, white bread(s), processed meats, and anything that is toxic to your body. There are many resources available online that you can navigate through to help you choose healthier options and inform you of not so healthy food choices. Here are a few I have used:

   • Dr. Colbert's Health Library: http://www.drcolbert .com/health-library.html

- Women's Health guidelines for "How to Eat for Health": http://womenshealth.gov/fitness -nutrition/how-to-eat-for-health/

- Let's Move guidelines, "Eat Healthy": http://www .letsmove.gov/eat-healthy

3. Research some yummy recipes and have fun creating a menu that will keep you coming back for more.

4. This requires a conscious effort on your part. No worries, you are not alone. God is with you on this journey.

5. Stay focused. You will soon realize that you feel so good you won't want to return to the old eating choices.

PRAYER

Dear God,

I am not afraid. I know You are with me. Thank You for helping me with the changes that are taking place. This is not easy, Lord, but I am committed to preparing my temple for the assignment You have given me. I trust You, Lord. Amen.

Day 6

YOU LOOK MARVELOUS!

I praise you, for I am fearfully and wonderfully made.
Wonderful are your works; my soul knows it very well.

《 PSALM 139:14, ESV 》

THERE IS GREAT power in declaring the Word of God over your life. There are wonderful things about you. Sometimes the enemy wants us to spend our days looking at all that is wrong about ourselves; however, I want you to know that in God's eyes, "You look marvelous!"

CHALLENGE

1. Make an affirmation and recite today's scripture three times—morning, afternoon, and evening: "I praise You, for I am fearfully and wonderfully made. Wonderful are Your works; my soul knows it very well."

2. Write at least five things that are wonderful about you.

3. Quiet the voices of negative things said about you and focus on how great God has created you to be.

PRAYER

Dear God,

Sometimes I don't feel good about myself. May I never forget that it is You who formed and created me. Therefore, I affirm that I have been "fearfully and wonderfully" made. Thank You, Lord, for creating me for greatness. Amen!

Day 7

DEAR ME

Examine yourselves, to see whether you are in the faith. Test yourselves. Or do you not realize this about yourselves, that Jesus Christ is in you?—unless indeed you fail to meet the test!

《 2 CORINTHIANS 13:5, ESV 》

L ET ME ASK you a question: If you could write a letter to yourself, what would it say? More importantly, what would you discover?

CHALLENGE

1. Write a letter to yourself.

2. Take a few minutes to examine yourself—spiritually and emotionally.

3. Start writing, and as you write, don't stop to make corrections. You will be the only one reading your letter. It is important to keep writing until you feel you are done.

4. Now read it to yourself.

5. What did you discover?

PRAYER

Dear God,

As I take on this challenge, I ask You to examine my heart and show me the areas in my life You would like me to work on. Sometimes I get so busy that I neglect to see what is most often obvious to others. Today, I open up my heart to self-discovery as Your Spirit guides me. I surrender it all to You, Lord. Amen!

Day 8

DO YOU REMEMBER WHAT YOU ATE YESTERDAY?

So, whether you eat or drink, or whatever you do, do all to the glory of God.

《 1 CORINTHIANS 10:31, ESV 》

KEEPING A FOOD diary may seem like a chore and more work. But what if I told you that keeping a food diary can help you lose weight, stay focused, expose eating habits and patterns, and promote discipline? In addition, it holds you accountable to yourself.

CHALLENGE

1. Start by creating or downloading a food journal from the Internet. A smartphone food journal app works well too.

2. After each food intake, log what you ate. Somewhere near it write how you were feeling before you ate. For example, were you happy, sad, stressed, or anxious?

3. Each evening, after your last entry, look at your day's intake as well as your emotional status. Journal your discoveries and write any changes you would like to make.

4. Repeat the process the next day and for the remainder of the challenge; see what you discover about yourself.

PRAYER

Dear God,

Lead me as I commit to today's challenge. Help me to make food choices that are right and will honor and glorify You. Keep me from all unhealthy food choices, and let Your conviction stir me onto the right path. Amen.

Day 9

I MAY JUST LIKE THIS!

Therefore, if anyone is in Christ, he is a new creation.
The old has passed away; behold, the new has come.

《 2 CORINTHIANS 5:17, ESV 》

I CONFESS: I AM a creature of habit. In the past I would have never thought of venturing out of my comfort zone to try new things, let alone eat something that looked like it belonged anywhere else but the kitchen. Yet I have discovered there are so many wonderful and healthy choices out there. Every time I try something new that I know is good for me, I feel accomplished and transported into a world of treasures previously unknown to me! Are you ready to try something new?

CHALLENGE

1. Whether you go out for dinner or stay in, I challenge you to try something you have never tried before.

2. Think of something that is healthy and good for you, and give it a bite! Options could include a new vegetable, fish, fruit, grain, and so on.

3. If great change is going to occur, your taste buds may have to change. No worries, they will adjust. Give it time.

PRAYER

Dear God,

As I venture out into unfamiliar territory, help me to keep an open mind and an open heart. I know You love me, Lord, and with Your guidance and direction I will overcome my fears and walk in obedience as I walk into the unknown. My senses were created by You. I will surrender them to You. Amen.

Day 10

WE NEED EACH OTHER

Two are better than one, because they have a good reward for their toil. For it they fall, one will lift up his fellow. But woe to him who is alone when he falls and has not another to lift him up!

« ECCLESIASTES 4:9–10, ESV »

I AM GOING TO let you in on a little secret. I thought I could do it on my own, but I can't. Neither can you. Every time I come up against a roadblock, I call a prayer team. I call the first people who come to mind as the Lord leads, people I know are serious about prayer. Can I tell you? *It works.* So next time you are in trouble or need God to intervene, pick up the phone or send a group text to at least two or three people who you know will stop everything and pray right then and there. He hasn't failed me yet!

CHALLENGE

1. Select a circle of friends. You can start with two or three friends who have a prayer life and are consistent.

2. Ask them if they would commit to pray for you in times of need. This is what I call "the spiritual 911" prayer line.

3. If you find yourself stressed, anxious, concerned, fearful, or battling, you can get in touch with this select group and ask them to pray.

4. Thank them. Feeling confident that as you go forth in your assignment you have the assurance of knowing

you are not alone can get you through the worst of days.

PRAYER

Dear God,

Thank You for divine connections, covenant relationships, and praying partners. I know I don't have to carry the burden alone. As You lead, I will count on others to help pray me through. Amen!

Day 11

INTRODUCING ME

For we are his workmanship, created in Christ Jesus for good works, which God prepared beforehand, that we should walk in them.

« EPHESIANS 2:10, ESV »

CREATE A COLLAGE. It is an art form composed of pictures, cutouts, magazine photographs, paper, and so on that you lay out on a sheet of paper or poster board. Collages are a form of self-expression and a way for you to sit, relax, create, and focus on who you are as an individual. There are so many wonderful things about us, yet we often miss the little things that make us wonderful.

CHALLENGE

1. You will need construction paper (any color), old magazines you have read, and a glue stick. If you are into scrapbooking, bring out your kit!

2. Create a collage as if you were introducing yourself to someone without having to speak. It would be a visual introduction. (Include spiritual, emotional, and physical components.)

3. Get creative. Use pictures, cut-up letters, glitter, and anything else you can think of. Make it as creative and beautiful as possible.

4. When you are finished, step back and look at it. How did you feel creating this collage? Is your assignment a part of the collage? Do you see yourself?

PRAYER

Dear God,

I want others to see the work You are doing in my life. I know You are not finished with me. I will continue to walk in obedience as You continue to mold and shape me. Amen.

Day 12

WALK IT OUT

For the moment all discipline seems painful rather than pleasant, but later it yields the peaceful fruit of righteousness to those who have been trained by it. Therefore lift your drooping hands.

« HEBREWS 12:11–12, ESV »

WHAT KIND OF day are you having? Are you feeling like you don't have what it takes to make it through? Go for a walk with God.

CHALLENGE

1. Go for a fifteen-minute to half-hour walk.

2. While you walk, take some time and have a one-on-one conversation with God. Trust me. He is listening.

3. Speak your mind. Talk with God. Release your emotions, thoughts, and cares.

4. Your objective is to pull those thoughts and emotions *out* of you and give them to Him. Try it. You will feel lighter and more able to continue your journey.

PRAYER

Dear God,
Just when I think I have it together, something goes off course and it feels like I am back to square one. Becoming disciplined isn't easy, but I know I must do

what is right in Your sight. I take comfort in knowing that during these times I can get away from it all and run to You. Amen!

Day 13

STOP, REFLECT, LISTEN, AND PROCEED

But the Helper, the Holy Spirit, whom the Father will send in my name, he will teach you all things and bring to your remembrance all that I have said to you.

« JOHN 14:26, ESV »

SOME TIME AGO I remember having worked a long day. Since I had not yet had dinner, I had some decisions to make. The first question was, should I eat? The answer, of course, was yes. Next, what do I eat? Well, the thoughtless reaction was to eat whatever came to mind, based on habits. For example, at dinners we eat full meals. But because I stopped, focused, reflected, and listened to my body and the spirit inside me, I was able to take control and order what was best for this temple.

CHALLENGE

This is how the Holy Spirit works. We have decisions to make, and sometimes we act on habit and impulse. What would happen if every decision was measured first by stopping, then reflecting, and finally listening to what the Spirit of God was telling us?

1. Before deciding what you are going to eat, stop, reflect, and listen, then proceed to sustain your body.

2. Write down how difficult or how easy this exercise was for you.

PRAYER

Dear God,

I have to confess: sometimes I want comfort food. Yet I know I can't act on impulse. Help me as I stop, listen, and reflect on my eating choices. I am determined to finish strong. Amen.

Day 14

YOUR WORD IS A
LAMP UNTO MY FEET

Your word is a lamp to my feet and a light for my path.
« PSALM 119:105 »

Did you know we have a GPS (Global Positioning System) we can use when we are lost and can't see where we are going? Yes, the Word of God is certainly a lamp unto our feet. I can't tell you how many times I have used my GPS, and before long, I find myself where I am supposed to be. I have reached my destination.

CHALLENGE

1. Set apart a specific time today to read one of your favorite chapters in the Bible.

2. Stop often and reflect. What is God revealing to you regarding your assignment?

3. Get your journal and write down the revelation you received from this reading.

PRAYER

Dear God,
May I find the answers I have been searching for, and may I be strengthened by the power of Your Word. May it guide me in the right path. Amen.

CHANGE YOUR STINKING THINKING

Finally, brothers, whatever is true, whatever is honorable, what is just, whatever is pure, whatever is lovely, whatever is commendable, if there is any excellence, if there is anything worthy of praise, think about these things.

« PHILIPPIANS 4:8, ESV »

HAVE YOU EVER had a random thought that you are certain is not part of God's plan? For example, "God can't use someone like me," or, "I am not smart enough or pretty enough." These are unexpected but often recurring thoughts that can destroy our assignment if we continue to feed them.

CHALLENGE

1. Write in your journal three lingering thoughts you want to change that you know affect the way you see yourself.

2. What would you like to change about these thoughts before the challenge is over?

3. Make a plan and execute it.

PRAYER

Dear God,
I know that anything ugly and negative doesn't come from You. Today I bring to You these thoughts that make

me sad and angry... (fill in your emotions). I give all my junk to You, and I do away with my negative thinking. Help me to implement Your Word to protect myself from these thoughts making my mind their home again. In Jesus's name I pray, amen.

Day 16

THE EXTRA MILE

But he said to me, "My grace is sufficient for you, for my power is made perfect in weakness."

« 2 CORINTHIANS 12:9, ESV »

OK, PERHAPS YOU are like me and find any excuse not to exercise. Yet it's something we need to do if we are going to be wholly fit. So why not get the workout in every chance we can, right?

CHALLENGE

1. Today you will take the stairs rather than an elevator.

2. Wherever you go today, don't park your car near the entrance. Make a conscious choice to park farther so that you may walk more.

3. If you are used to walking, then challenge your mind and actions to do things out of your normal routine.

PRAYER

Dear God,

I must confess: there are things I know are good for me that I don't like to do. However, I know that obedience makes room for promotion; therefore, will You give me the strength and the desire to continue forth so I may give the very best of me? Thank You, Lord, for being patient with me. Amen.

LET'S CELEBRATE!

I am the LORD your God, who brought you up out of the land of Egypt. Open your mouth wide, and I will fill it.

《 PSALM 81:10, ESV 》

How EXCITING TO know that God has delivered us from so many things and He is doing a good work in us. He has brought us out of old habits and modes of thinking, and today we are walking in absolute newness. Well, OK, He isn't finished with us yet, but why not celebrate?

CHALLENGE

1. Plan a celebratory meal (with moderation, of course; you don't want to regress).

2. Gather your family or close friends and share the meal while you talk about your progress, the changes you are seeing, and the goodness of God in your life.

3. While you are eating, think of all the wonderful things you have experienced in this journey thus far. Enjoy each bite, and take your time eating. This is your moment. You deserve it. You have come this far!

PRAYER

Dear God,
    Wow! I can't believe I have come this far. You sure are amazing and faithful. Thank You for not giving up

on me. I am committed to enduring until the end! I am pressing toward the mark, and I will have the victory because You are my strong tower. Amen.

Day 18

YOU HAVE A DATE TONIGHT

You make known to me the path of life; in your presence there is fullness of joy; at your right hand are pleasures forevermore.

« PSALM 16:11, ESV »

Some of the greatest conversations I've had have been with God. I remember a time when I really went out of my way to set the atmosphere. I invited God to join me in the conversation and discovered that in His presence there truly is complete fullness of joy.

CHALLENGE

1. Set a time today to spend with God.

2. Set the atmosphere. Light a candle, play some worship music, and rid yourself of all distractions. It's a date with God.

3. Invite God to sit with you and just spend time in conversation with Him. Take time to speak, but take time to listen as well. He will speak to your inner being.

PRAYER

Dear God,

Today I invite You to join me for a time of conversation. Fill me with Your presence and peace. May I walk away with a greater understanding of the depth of Your love and purpose for my life. Amen.

Day 19

MAKE THE CALL

Be kind to one another, tenderhearted...
« EPHESIANS 4:32, ESV »

WHEN WAS THE last time you called someone and told them how amazing they are or how much they have blessed you? Did you know that blessing others with kind words is good for your soul? When you lift someone's spirit with kind words, your spirit is nurtured as well.

CHALLENGE

1. Think of someone you appreciate wholeheartedly.

2. Make a phone call (no texts, please). Let the person hear your voice.

3. Tell that person how wonderful they are, or perhaps that you appreciate their friendship or the manner in which they bless others....You get the point.

PRAYER

Dear God,
Thank You for the wonderful people You have placed in my life. I know at times I am not the easiest person to get along with. Somehow You always send someone who reminds me of Your love and care for me. You are one awesome God. Your blessings over my life are infinite, and I am forever grateful. Amen.

IS IT TIME FOR A CHECKUP?

For I will restore health to you, and your wounds I will heal, declares the LORD.

« JEREMIAH 30:17, ESV »

WHEN WAS THE last time you went to the doctor and had a complete physical? If we are going to be fully fit, our health matters.

CHALLENGE

1. Make an appointment today to get a complete physical.

2. Take time to listen to your body. What is it telling you?

3. Write down some things you would like to discuss with your doctor that may be of concern to you.

4. Trust God and do not fear. He is your Creator and is with you every step of the way.

PRAYER

Dear God,

I admit I have been so busy that I have not made time to care for me. Thank You for Your Word that always convicts me to change. I am reminded today that I cannot be so busy that I neglect important responsibilities such as my health. Thank You for leading me to a healthy lifestyle. Amen.

Day 21

BEWARE OF TRAPS

The Lord will rescue me from every evil attack.

« 2 TIMOTHY 4:18 »

Y OU HAVE BEEN doing well on your challenge and want to reward yourself with a piece of pie or a nice big, juicy steak. Wait! Are you ready? Is this what your body is telling you it needs, or is this a trap to awaken the old appetites?

CHALLENGE

1. Write down three ways you would reward yourself for eating healthily and sticking to the challenge.

2. If food is one of the ways, write down which food and why you chose it.

3. Think about the potential effects you will endure after the consumption of this particular food, and write them down.

4. Remember, there is a reason why a trap is called a trap.

PRAYER

Dear God,

Thank You for keeping me alert to the traps of the enemy. I have come too far to mess this up now. I am more than a conqueror. Help me to be proactive and not reactive. Keep Your spirit alive in me as it convicts me of the choices I make. I trust You, Lord. Amen.

Day 22

SPIRITUAL ALIGNMENT

Abide in me, and I in you. As the branch cannot bear fruit by itself, unless it abides in the vine, neither can you, unless you abide in me.

《 JOHN 15:4, ESV 》

W E ALL HAVE areas that need to be aligned. Do you know your area(s)? Is it a better prayer life, more discipline, devotional time, inner healing, or organization?

CHALLENGE

1. Make a list of three things you want to align in your life.

2. Create a course of action that can help you get started immediately on becoming aligned.

3. Present your list to the Lord and invite Him to lead you.

PRAYER

Dear God,

I thank You because today You remind me that I need to be spiritually aligned in certain areas of my life. I confess that at times it is not easy to change, yet I know if I am willing, You will meet me at the point of my need. I invite You to lead me through this process, and may I continue forth victorious. Amen.

Day 23

RELATIONSHIPS MATTER

And God saw that the light was good. And God separated the light from the darkness.

« GENESIS 1:4, ESV »

LAUNDRY IS NOT my favorite thing to do. I don't like the process of separating the dark colors from the light colors. I have learned my lesson one too many times. I have mixed colors together only to have the clothes ruined by my lack of patience. It reminds me of our relationships. We think we can mix them all together and treat them all the same. God wants us to sort out our relationships and separate the dark (those that may be harmful) from the light (those that nurture your God-given destiny). Otherwise, some may end up ruined in the mix.

CHALLENGE

1. Make a list of your most precious relationships.

2. Write down what is unique about each of them.

3. Find ways to appreciate their uniqueness.

4. Find ways to set boundaries between the good relationships and those that may be harmful.

PRAYER

Dear God,

Thank You for my friends. We all need people in our lives. Sometimes I forget that each carries his or her own uniqueness, and I treat them the same way. Help me to see the gifts in each of my friends. In Jesus's name I pray, amen.

GET ORGANIZED

But all things should be done decently and in order.

《 1 CORINTHIANS 14:40, ESV 》

IS THERE A closet, a drawer, a room, or a garage that you have been wanting to clean out and organize but haven't? You just haven't felt the passion or commitment to do so? Well, today is your day. Today you can get your workout getting organized. Are you ready?

CHALLENGE

1. Pick a room, a closet, a couple of drawers, or even a section of the garage that needs cleaning and organizing.

2. Give yourself a time to start and to finish, as this will get you to move at a speed that will promote physical stamina.

3. When you are finished, write in your journal the feelings, thoughts, and emotions you observe after the completion of this challenge.

PRAYER

Dear God,

You are a God of order. I thank You because I can feel You working in many areas of my life. I know that chaos can promote negative emotions. Unstable emotions are dangerous, as they can affect the assignment over my life. It feels good to know that You are in this with me. Thank You. Amen.

Day 25

ARE YOU AN EMOTIONAL EATER?

Many are the plans in the mind of a man, but it is the purpose of the LORD that will stand.

« PROVERBS 19:21, ESV »

DURING THE TIME I was engrossed in my own thirty-day challenge (yes, I will not ask you to do anything I haven't done), I realized, through my food log, that I was an emotional eater. I ate when I was feeling stressed or bored. Having an awareness of this allowed me to possess greater control of my emotions and submit my concerns to the Lord. Every time I want to eat, I ask myself, "Why do you want to eat now?"

CHALLENGE

1. Look through your food log and make a list of the times you ate more than you should have.

2. Check your emotional state for each time you overate.

3. Write down what patterns you observe and what you want to change.

4. Submit your concerns to the Lord in prayer.

PRAYER

Dear God,
Oftentimes I am an emotional mess and run to food for comfort. This is not what I should be doing. Teach me to run to You in these times, as I know I can depend on You to help me. Today I pause to listen and make the right choices. Amen.

Day 26

WHAT HAVE YOU BEEN AVOIDING?

So whoever knows the right thing to do and fails to do it, for him it is sin.

« JAMES 4:17, ESV »

IS THERE SOMETHING you have been avoiding that you know God is telling you to confront? Maybe it's ignoring a certain area in your life. Perhaps it's not being able to forgive someone who may have hurt you.

CHALLENGE

1. Take an honest assessment of what you have been avoiding.

2. Write in your journal what it is that you must confront.

3. Create a course of action and ask God for courage to proceed. This will not be easy, which is most likely why you have been ignoring it. But with God's help, you can do it!

PRAYER

Dear God,

This is a very painful challenge, as there are very painful things I'd rather not talk about. Yet I know that if I am going to have complete healing, I must deal with this area in my life. Give me the courage and peace needed to move forward with this challenge. In Jesus's name, amen.

Day 27

YOU ARE IMMOVABLE

Therefore, my beloved brothers, be steadfast, immovable, always abounding in the work of the Lord, knowing that in the Lord your labor is not in vain.

« 1 CORINTHIANS 15:58, ESV »

YOU ARE ALMOST at the end of the thirty-day challenge. Perhaps you had moments of wanting to stop. Maybe you did, but decided to pick it back up. Great! You are still here, and this speaks volumes of your commitment in becoming fit for your assignment.

CHALLENGE

1. Take a moment to reflect on this thirty-day journey.

2. Write in your journal what days were the most challenging and why.

3. Read what you have just discovered about yourself.

4. Thank God for the changes, and make up your mind to continue the journey to wholeness.

PRAYER

Dear God,

I thank You because You have brought me this far. You truly are an awesome God. There were days that were more difficult than others and I thought of giving up, but You sustained me. I know I possess the strength to continue steadfast. I owe it all to You, Lord. Thank You for loving me unconditionally. Amen.

Day 28

LET'S DANCE

For you have need of endurance, so that when you have done the will of God you may receive what is promised.

« HEBREWS 10:36, ESV »

HERE IS A fact: exercise works. Exercise promotes endurance, in addition to its many other benefits. So as much as we may want to run from it, we need to run to it and make it a part of our lives—part of the assignment over our lives. So with that said, why not have fun?

CHALLENGE

1. Gather up your family tonight and create a space where everyone can move freely. (There is no age limit.)

2. Pick some fun music the entire family enjoys.

3. Set the clock for a half hour of exercise.

4. Start the music and have each family member take turns in creating a freestyle dance routine on the spot that the entire family must follow. (Be prepared for lots of laughter and fun while burning calories.)

PRAYER

Dear God,

Thank You for providing me with the endurance to finish what I started. I know I will receive what has been promised. I will be fit for my assignment. Amen.

NATURE-ALL (NATURAL) FEAST

The heart of a man plans his way, but the LORD
establishes his steps.

« PROVERBS 16:9, ESV »

ISN'T IT WONDERFUL to know that the Lord establishes our
steps? He cares for all areas of our lives. He created animals and
planted gardens so we would enjoy the very best of nature. Trust
me when I tell you, He wants us fit for our assignment in our food
choices as well. Let's enjoy some of God's very best!

CHALLENGE

1. Gather your family together and plan a salad buffet
   for dinner.

2. Have each family member pick a healthy food item.

3. Pick a lean meat (chicken or fish).

4. Gather all your food items; include greens, beans,
   tomatoes, and more—the possibilities are endless.

5. Set up an area to look like a buffet table, and have
   everyone create his or her own salad. (This is a good
   opportunity to introduce your family to new food
   options.)

6. *Bon appetit!*

PRAYER

Dear God,

You think of everything. It is comforting to know that as Your children we do not lack anything, as You have provided all we need. Help me to be an example to my family as they walk in their assignment. May we establish eating patterns that will be pleasing to You. In Jesus's name, amen.

Day 30

PRESSING ON!

I press on toward the goal for the prize of the upward call of God in Christ Jesus.

« PHILIPPIANS 3:14, ESV »

YOU HAVE MADE it to the thirtieth day! You have spent thirty days in reflection, self-discovery, conviction, confrontation, revelation, and transformation. You have walked a journey of spiritual, mental, and physical alignment. I rejoice with you!

Here is one more challenge before you can begin to implement what was most useful to you and make it part of your everyday life.

CHALLENGE

1. Write a letter explaining what you believe is your assignment. In that letter write what you learned during the thirty days that made you ready to move forward with great confidence.

2. Read the letter to yourself and share it with a friend or family member.

3. Extract the areas on which you need to place ongoing focus.

4. Move forward with tenacity. Your assignment was created for you, and no one can be better at being you than YOU!

PRAYER

Lord,

I stand in awe of Your greatness. Thank You for the conviction via Your Word and the Holy Spirit. Thank You for helping me confront the areas of my life that needed confronting. I give You thanks for being a God of such grand revelation. You helped me to see the things I couldn't see for myself.

Thank You for the transformation that has taken place in my life. Let it forever bring You glory. Help me to continue this journey with passion and purpose, and allow the transformation in my life to serve as a testimony of what we all can do when we surrender to You. I declare that I will be fit for my assignment. In Jesus's name, amen.

NOTES

INTRODUCTION

1. The Free Dictionary, s.v. "confrontation," http://www
.thefreedictionary.com/confrontation (accessed January 23, 2014).

2. *Merriam-Webster Dictionary*, s.v. "transformation," http://www
.merriam-webster.com/dictionary/transformation (accessed January 23, 2014).

CHAPTER 1
YOU HAVE AN ASSIGNMENT

1. The Free Dictionary, s.v. "alignment," http://www.thefreedictionary
.com/alignment (accessed January 22, 2014).

2. ThinkExist.com, "Pieter V. Admiraal Quotes," http://thinkexist.com/
quotes/dr._pieter_v._admiraal/ (accessed December 29, 2013).

CHAPTER 2
YOUR BODY IS A TEMPLE

1. R. E. Hawkins, *Model for Guiding the Counseling Process* (Lynchburg,
VA: Liberty University, 2006).

CHAPTER 3
GETTING TO THE HEART OF THE MATTER

1. J. D. Douglas, *New International Bible Dictionary* (Grand Rapids,
MI: Zondervan Publishing House, 1999), s.v. "heart."

2. David Benner, *Desiring God's Will* (Downers Grove, IL: InterVarsity
Press, 2005).

3. Saint Augustine, *Confessions* (N.p.: Oxford University Press, 1999).

CHAPTER 5
CHANGE FROM THE INSIDE OUT

1. Ron Dicker, "Plastic Surgery Spending Is Up, As Number of Chin
Augmentation Surges," *Huffington Post*, April 18, 2012, http://www
.huffingtonpost.com/2012/04/18/plastic-surgery-spending-up-2011_n_
1435512.html (accessed January 23, 2014); "Minimally-Invasive, Facial
Rejuvenation Procedures Fuel 5 Percent Growth," PlasticSurgery.org,
http://www.plasticsurgery.org/news-and-resources/press-release-archives/
2013/14-million-cosmetic-plastic-surgery-procedures-performed-in-2012
(accessed January 23, 2014).

2. Temma Ehrenfeld, "Plastic Surgery Doesn't Boost Self-Esteem," *Open Gently* (blog), *Psychology Today*, December 10, 2012, http://www.psychologytoday.com/blog/open-gently/201212/plastic-surgery-doesnt-boost-self-esteem (accessed January 23, 2014).

CHAPTER 6
WHATEVER YOU DON'T CONTROL, CONTROLS YOU

1. Charles Haddon Spurgeon, *Morning and Evening* (Peabody, MA: Hendrickson Pub, 1991).

CHAPTER 7
STEP 1: CONVICTION

1. James Strong, *The New Strong's Complete Dictionary of Bible Words* (Nashville, TN: Thomas Nelson Publishers, 1996), s.v. "conviction."

2. Oswald Chambers, *My Utmost for His Highest*, Classic Edition, "Repentance," December 7, 2013, http://utmost.org/classic/repentance-classic/ (accessed January 23, 2014).

CHAPTER 8
STEP 2: CONFRONTATION

1. The Free Dictionary.com, s.v. "confront," http://www.thefreedictionary.com/confront (accessed January 22, 2014).

2. Joan Didion, *The Year of Magical Thinking* (New York: Alfred A. Knopf, 2005), 3.

3. C. S. Lewis, *The Problem of Pain* (London: The Centenary Press, 1940).

CHAPTER 9
STEP 3: REVELATION

1. Merriam-Webster.com, s.v. "revelation," http://www.merriam-webster.com/dictionary/revelation (accessed January 22, 2014).

2. As quoted in Cornelius Plantinga Jr., *Engaging God's World: A Christian Vision of Faith, Learning, and Living* (Grand Rapids, MI: Wm. B. Eerdmans Publishing Co., 2002), 7.

CHAPTER 10
STEP 4: TRANSFORMATION

1. Dictionary.com, s.v. "transformation," http://dictionary.reference.com/browse/transformation?s=t (accessed January 22, 2014).

CHAPTER 11
FINISH WHAT YOU STARTED

1. The Free Dictionary.com , s.v. "distraction," http://www
.thefreedictionary.com/distraction (accessed January 22, 2014).

FREE NEWSLETTERS
TO HELP EMPOWER YOUR LIFE

Why subscribe today?

❏ **DELIVERED DIRECTLY TO YOU.** All you have to do is open your inbox and read.

❏ **EXCLUSIVE CONTENT.** We cover the news overlooked by the mainstream press.

❏ **STAY CURRENT.** Find the latest court rulings, revivals, and cultural trends.

❏ **UPDATE OTHERS.** Easy to forward to friends and family with the click of your mouse.

CHOOSE THE E-NEWSLETTER THAT INTERESTS YOU MOST:

- Christian news
- Daily devotionals
- Spiritual empowerment
- And much, much more

SIGN UP AT: **http://freenewsletters.charismamag.com**

8178